The book you are holding in your hands is a work of love that was origi[nally] crafted, edited, and produced by Jacks Ashley McNamara and Sascha Altm[an] of 2004. This book is what we wished we'd had when we couldn't make sense of what was happening in our heads and no one else seemed to understand. We wish we'd had it when we were first diagnosed with bipolar disorder and were confused about what that meant; we wish we'd had it when we were 15 and freaked out and didn't know why we were so much more volatile than everyone else around us; we wish we'd had it when we were first getting out of the hospital and trying to figure out how to piece our lives back together; we wish we'd had it every time someone told us that we would never make it unless we made our dreams smaller and got a real job; we wish we'd had it when we didn't know anyone who'd been through this and could offer us a vision of life with mental illness that was full of possibility and wasn't full of walls.

This is the 10th Printing! Please turn to p. 82 & 83 for new postscript, reintroduction, and epilogue.

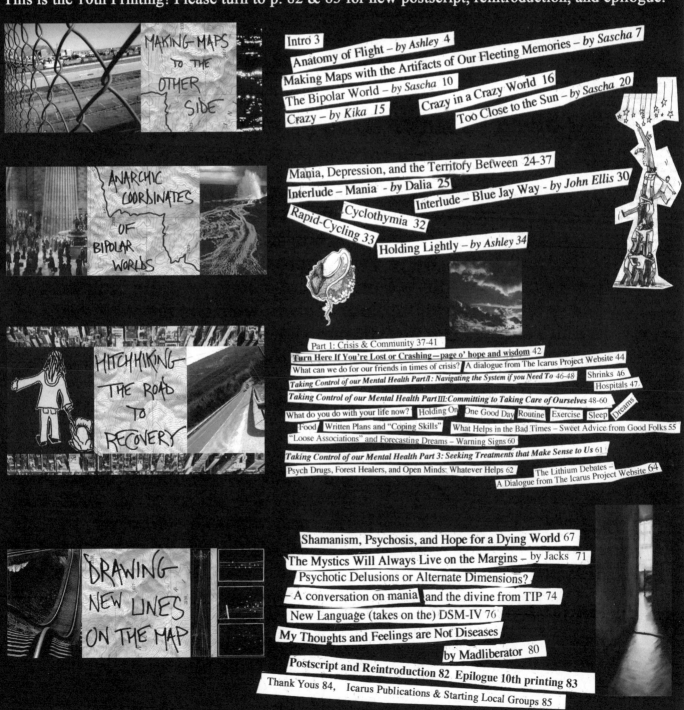

WE'RE GIVEN SO MANY MAPS OF HOW TO LIVE OUR LIVES

by the society we are raised in. Some of the maps are constructed by the shows we watch on television and the lessons we learn in classrooms; some are drawn up at our family kitchen tables and on our doctors' desks. We're very impressionable creatures; everything we experience leaves impressions on us. All the moments of pain and elation carve into our terrain with the crooked grace of rivers and ravines. The instructions we receive about how to cope, and what is good, are like roads across and into them.

MOST PEOPLE SEEM TO STICK TO THE ACCEPTED ROADS.

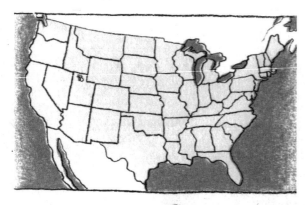

It's a scary thing to deviate from the path. But for so many of us, and especially for those of us with thin skin and drastic changes in our personal elevation, life is too hard to plot on a grid: the coordinates are always shifting. People like us don't have any choice but to figure out our own paths or be forever lost in land that never feels like home.

They tell us we are mentally ill. The two people putting together this reader you hold in your hands have been diagnosed with "Bipolar Disorder," the most recent medical language for what was once known as Manic Depression. It is considered a disease of the mind. The statistics are that 6 million people in the United States have some form of the disorder, and that 1 out of 5 people left untreated will eventually kill themselves. But this "illness" is more than a bunch of statistics, or a set of symptoms. For those of us who live with this awkward label, the phenomenon it describes is something fluid and hard to pin down, yet none of us can escape its effects on our lives. We share common patterns and eerily common stories, some devastating and some inspiring—and so few of them have actually been mapped.

Since we wrote this book 9 years ago our understanding of the complexities of using the term "bipolar disorder" has grown ever more nuanced. Please check out the epilogue on p. 83 for an update.

A simple place to start is here: we're sensitive. We feel things hard and fast. We feel things quiet and deep. We feel things huge and open. We feel things heavy and slow. Sometimes we feel too much and crash to a place where we don't feel anything at all; the walls of depression are so strong that they drown out sound and light like the cinderblocks of a psych ward cell locked up inside our souls. Sometimes we don't feel anything at all because we're so busy talking to angels or spies that we check out of what everyone else calls reality for a while. Sometimes we don't remember anything at all because we stepped out of line, got stuck on too many damn tranquilizers, and are drooling on ourselves in the Quiet Room somewhere. Sometimes we archive every last nanosecond of the world's most perfect afternoon in the infrastructure of our brains. Sometimes we feel nothing at all but pain. We've got thin skin. The world creeps under our fingernails and into our dreams.

And where do you go with that? Because the world's pretty crazy itself these days. Do you pour it into crooked little paintings and big-voiced songs? Do you drive too fast and scream at people who get in your way? Do you hide with it in bed or rage with it at work? Do you smother it with a martini or a prescription for Prozac? Do you wear it in a smile like an electric sunset or in a blank stare like a broken screen?

Do you turn for help to a doctor or a priest? To a witch or a Wal-Mart? What map do you follow?

In this little book we've assembled an atlas of maps, back and forth through the subconscious and consciousness, from hospital waiting rooms to collective house kitchens, from the desert to the supermarket. The pages we are giving to you chart some of the underground tunnels beneath the mainstream medical model of treatment, tunnels carved by brave and visionary people before us, and tunnels we're helping to carve ourselves with our friends. They go beyond three dimensions. They are maps made up of ideas and stories and examples from many people's lives. They are maps of our souls as well as the world outside. Some of these maps will help you to navigate through the existing architecture of the mental health establishment; some of them might help you figure out for yourself where you stand in relation to the larger ecosystem of the earth and the people who inhabit it.

We have drawn these maps from the members of The Icarus Project website, from letters and e-mails, and from our own lives. While we have tried to include a wide range of experience and a fascinating bunch of stories, please understand that this reader was compiled by two biased but good-hearted individuals, Sascha and Jacks, doing their best to gather together everything they wanted the world to know in the short span of two winter months. It is necessarily imperfect and intentionally subjective; we do not even want to pretend that we (or any of the "authorities," for that matter) have any objective knowledge of what bipolar disorder is. We're beginning by telling you a bit about what we know best: our own experiences with bipolar.

I always knew I was different; the world seemed to hit me so much harder and fill me so much fuller than anyone else I knew. Even as a little kid I was possessed by a need to write constantly, make tons of intricate drawings, and stay up all night reading or just thinking about how intoxicating and painful everything was. Slanted sunlight could make me dizzy with its beauty and witnessing unkindness made me feel physical pain. I was pretty sure I was "crazy" by the time I was 11, when the twisted black nights and the depressions came on, but I didn't have any words for it or anyone to tell. When I was 14 I got interested in words. I remember laying in bed one night, wide awake with the hallway light bulb buzzing under my skin as everyone else dreamed peacefully, wishing for some sleep after another exhausting few weeks of wild-eyed electricity and secret, hysterical sobbing. Nothing in particular had happened except that no one could understand all the rapture and rage in my head. I started wondering about this word I'd read: manic depression. It was used to describe some poet in an English book. It sounded drastic and terrifying and even though I didn't really know what it was I had an irrational hunch that it might describe me. But of course I didn't talk to talk to anyone about it. I just laid awake for a long time.

5 years later I got diagnosed with bipolar disorder, the latest term for manic depression, in a Virginia psych ward. The day before the nurses had found me swinging from curtains, screaming, after cutting up my arms to make sure I was still capable of feeling anything. I wasn't sure if I was real anymore; the depression seemed to saturate every inch of my soul. Three months before I'd been euphorically convinced for weeks that I possessed the one shining piece of knowledge that could end planetary injustice and liberate us all. Now I found myself in the proverbial padded room, being forced to swallow tranquilizers when all I wanted was music. The next day my doctor, an old white man with about as much compassion as a doornail and a distressing number of frown lines, entered my room with the comment "cutting yourself is a nasty little habit for good girls like you because it leaves scars." This man was supposed to heal me. He was supposed to be my hope. A vague old impulse in the back of my head wanted to kick his ass, but mostly I hated myself so much at the time that I just felt a creeping shame. And I wanted so badly to believe what he said; he was supposed to have the magic key that would fix this broken mess I'd become, and I wanted that key more than anything on the face of the earth. When he told me it seemed like I was probably Bipolar Type II and started listing off diagnostic criteria from the DSM-IV that actually seemed to describe the patterns of my life, I was grateful. It was a relief, really, to think that there was a biological basis for all these behavior patterns that had been alternately fantastic and so incredibly difficult to live with, that had made most people in my life think I was this inspiring, creative, grab-life-by-the-horns kind of woman who had no idea how to handle herself and ended up being a total wreck as much as she was a superhero. It was a relief to think that all of this misery was not because I was just weak or difficult, which had been my family's take all along.

But what did these words mean when I went back out into the world? How would they change the way people saw me? What on earth would I do now? I had never known anyone diagnosed with a mental illness, or anyone who admitted to taking psych drugs. I remember staring out those psych ward windows that do not open and wondering bleakly if I would recognize myself once I started taking this handful of pink pills that was supposed to make me normal. I remember wondering if I was just giving up and selling my soul or if I was jumping on the boat to salvation. Mostly I remember wondering where the hell to go from there.

Because the map they gave me was terrifying. It was something like this: You will take psychiatric medication for the rest of your life. You will need to see a doctor constantly and always be on the lookout for side-effects. We will test your blood and your kidneys and your liver function every 3 months. You must have health insurance. You will need to live in one place. You must describe your disorder to all your friends and family, and they will watch over you, and you must trust all of our authority over your own, because you are not trustworthy. You will go to bed at a reasonable hour and get 8 hours of sleep every night and if you don't we will need to put you on more drugs. You should try to have a steady job, but you might not ever be able to, because this is a serious disability. And if you don't follow these instructions you will be totally out of control and it will just get worse and worse. People like you are dangerous if left untreated. Don't be one of the ones who has to be hospitalized over and over again. Trust me, I've read the studies and you haven't.

Once my head cleared enough to think again, I didn't trust the doctors further than I could throw them. It just seemed like they had no visceral knowledge of what I was experiencing. They could anatomize it with all the words they learned in books, the way you could anatomize the movement of bones and muscles that allows a bird to fly, but they had no idea what flight is all about.

And the moments when I'd been soaring with eyes full of horizon and a heart branded like a contour map with the outlines of rocky sunrises and the fractal branching of so many threads of understanding... these seemed like the most important

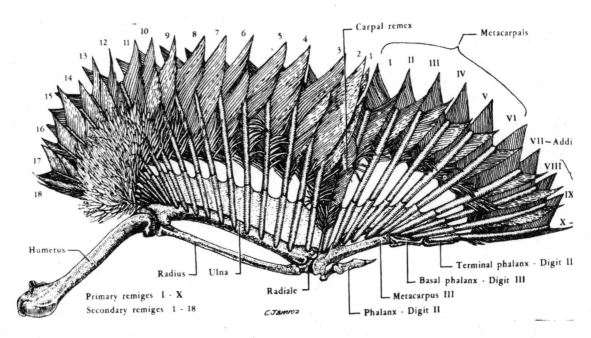

moments of my life. I didn't want to chalk them up to pathology, give them ugly labels like mania and delusion that seemed to invalidate them, make them less real. I didn't want to eradicate them all for the sake of "stability."

But doctors were not very interested in these arguments. The research made it very clear that I was supposed to comply with treatment. As I gradually regained my ability to read (paradoxically made possible, I have absolutely no doubt, by their drugs), I started to investigate the literature around bipolar disorder myself, and the more I read the more it seemed to me that doctors were trained to dissect people's lives into terms, classes, rules, cases, neurotransmitters, algorithms, atypical anti-psychotics, treatment-resistance, non-compliance... which seemed like a ridiculous approach to understanding a human being. And simply taking pink pills seemed like an incredibly reductive approach to healing a problematic personality, or whatever this was that I had. Yet as much as I resisted their words, they were all I could find, and over and over again these incredibly limited, awkward words seemed like the barest blueprints to my soul. And they could be found in the public library or on the internet... I hated the idea but also wondered, secretly, if there was some universality there. Obviously, if these words in big books in the library seemed to clumsily get at the flight patterns underlying my existence, there had to be other people with similar patterns.

free

Until I found them I worked in silence on my own map, which began with getting out of Virginia and out of my depressing day program full of washed up middle-aged men who'd spent most of their adulthood cycling in and out of various hospitals and abandoning all hope. My doctors protested furiously that I was not ready for independent life, but as soon as I felt like I could drive a hundred miles and maintain an occasional façade of functionality I finagled a job training horses and living by myself in a one room cottage in rural New Jersey. Endless group therapy and institutionalized relapse-prevention did not equate to healing for me; what soothed me was slowly drinking warm glasses of tea early in the morning by an east-facing window, watching the sunrise over my tiny, quiet house, and walking through the perfect frozen air to a warm barn full of waking horses and sensible smells like mud and wood. I refused therapy but took my drugs and let the narrative of my history and that huge question, *what went wrong*, unwind around me during the hours I spent cleaning stalls and feeding animals.

By the time I met Sascha years later I didn't talk much about being bipolar. I'd driven all my earthly possessions to California and gone off medication, struggling alone with the whole question of how to handle this fragile fire in my brain. My new friends had never seen me crazy, and I secretly hoped the whole thing had been a fluke. I'd spent the previous years moving from New Jersey to Greece to San Francisco, learning to paint and how to cook chard, never holding down that steady job or getting exactly the right amount of sleep, having weeks of brilliance and weeks of debilitating doubt, deciding to heal myself through food, or yoga, or mountains, all of this to the chagrin of various shrinks, who always insisted it was a dangerous idea for me to travel, or move, or take fewer drugs. I eventually abandoned them entirely. The map those doctors had drawn for me did a very effective job scaring me away from the whole mental health establishment and I had yet to meet anyone with flight patterns like mine who could give me a few clues.

And then Sascha published an article called "The Bipolar World" in the San Francisco Bay Guardian that I could relate to more than almost any piece of writing I've seen in my life. Once we met and started pouring out our life stories I realized that what I'd been trying to ignore, this way of being that gets labeled bipolar disorder, this framework of filters and illuminations through which I experience life, is actually more fundamental to how I exist in the world than I could ever have guessed. Because here was this stranger sitting on my bed and he could finish my sentences, could articulate the inner folds of my consciousness though we'd never even met because there was something so similar about the way our minds worked. And I was absolutely fascinated to find out what kind of maps he'd followed through his life.

We began The Icarus Project as a way of creating a space for people to share their trajectories through this under-charted world of blackness and brilliance and the million shades of gray that the medical establishment has no idea how to describe. We hoped it would help people feel less alone and begin to understand the layers of who they have been and who they can be. There are so many possibilities. Until I began this project, I was never sure I could get a handle on my sanity long enough to pull off one of the zillion visionary ideas in my head. In one of the ironies of this "illness," I probably never would have decided to take on the enormous task of learning to build a website from scratch while painting constantly, taking 5 classes, planting a garden, studying Buddhism, paying rent, etc. etc., without the adamant optimism and unfathomable energy of an unmedicated mania. But I probably wouldn't be here to continue the work if I hadn't gone back on medicine to tame the suicidal agitation I crashed into a month later. Patching together all these strange territories, my moods and my history, my lithium and my politics, my rent and my art, has been so confusing and painful at times that I have wanted to crawl out of my skin and disappear completely. It has required so much imagination. But it has also been penetrated throughout with a peculiar beauty, like grass busting up out of the sidewalk, and unimagined moments of grace, like last Valentine's Day, when I got an e-card from one of the Icarus Project folks. He called me a guardian angel. The doctors never charted moments like that on their maps.

Volatile adj. having a high vapor pressure and a low boiling point;
(of circumstances) liable to sudden, unpredictable, or explosive change
[ETYMOLOGY: from Latin volatilis flying, from volare **to fly**]

"To lose the scar of knowledge is to renew the wound." - Wendell Berry

"The rings around Saturn are its own shattered moons." - Jane LeCroy

Making Maps with the Artifacts of Our Fleeting Memories
or On Being a Time Traveler

by sascha scatter

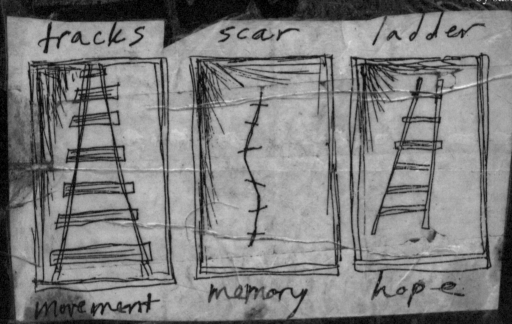

tracks   scar   ladder

movement   memory   hope

In traditional Hopi language, there's no past, present, or future in the grammar structure - different objects and people have different "states of becoming." It's a way of conceiving TIME that is completely unlike the one with which we've all grown up. This idea has always resonated with me and captured my imagination—maybe it's because of the non-linear nature of my mind and the blessing or curse I carry of feeling things strong and synchronous. As someone struggling with what is known these days, in the early part of the 21st Century, as bipolar disorder, it often becomes very clear to me that we don't all move at the same speeds or experience the same versions of reality. Even though we are all supposedly living under the same conventions of linear time, there are other things happening that are much harder to describe, much harder to grasp and hold on to with the language we are given to make sense of our lives.

The world inside my head sometimes feels like a carnival sideshow trickster game—full of smoke and mirrors, warping and shaping history through various gradations of manic and depressive lenses.

When I'm manic I feel like I have powers to see right through the things around me. I can't help noticing that the world is ending—but my mind screws up the calculations and thinks that the world is ending RIGHT NOW. When I'm depressed the television seems like it's broadcasting Live From Hell on all the channels. Time has stopped and I'm trapped in the worst nightmare I can possibly dream up for eternity. When I'm really down it's so easy for me to forget any good I've ever done and rewrite myself as a miserable pathetic fool and my life as a shameful tragedy that never should have happened. But when I'm up it seems like the entire universe is behind me, and not only have I worked out the perfect plans for the future of the earth--I have the energy to carry them out ...for the rest of the planets after that.

Unbeknownst to me, right around the corner all my plans are destined to crumble and I'm going to find myself wandering alone in the streets with the broken pieces, wondering how I ever had the imagination to dream them all up and the chutzpah to actually believe they might happen. It's a strange universe I inhabit: my past is never fixed, it seems to bend with the force of the present. Even when my life is the most steady and my internal pendulum is swinging closer to center, all my experiences are still informed by everything I've seen through these eyes, everything I've felt with this heart—and everything that, at some point, I believed to be real.

Because this territory in my internal universe is continually shifting, I've learned to look for patterns and rhythms in the chaos that I can use as guides when I can't locate steady ground. So I make maps from my memories. I make my maps out of words and stories.

I keep a written journal, and anyone who knows me knows that my big black book goes with me everywhere. It lies at the edge of my mattress next to my head, every night, with an open pen nestled in its crevice, waiting for me to wake up and scribble down my dreams. My journal books are cut and paste patchworks layered with different pieces of my life: my own words interspersed between flyers from events, seed packets, photos of friends and loved ones, collages of torn apart and reworked advertisements, dried leaves, maps of towns and cities, newspaper and magazine clippings, postcards, and scribbled contact info and little drawings from the people I meet. My journals are multilayered metaphorically and physically. Sometimes if I write something that I can't bear to look at because it's too embarrassing or complicated, I'll paste over it with a photo or a flyer and know I can go back and read it when I'm ready, whether it's a week later or in three years when I rediscover its beckoning pages calling to me from the shelf.

Above my desk the big black journals sit next to one another, held together with duct tape and sweat and train grease and gluestick glue. They document the last 9 years of my life--the years since I dropped out of college--in case I have trouble making sense of where I've been; they're something I can refer back to when I'm trying to figure out where I've been. I can trace my dreams and my waking hours back almost a decade and find deeper insight into myself with every passing year.

8

My journals are the maps of this crazy journey.

They look like the rings of a tree in the history they tell by their appearance. The books I've kept as I was breaking down in psychosis are tattered shreds and barely held together, showing evidence of trauma the same way the inner rings of a tree from a year of fires will be darker and more charred. My handwriting changes between my mania and my depression -- excited sentences taking up enormous spaces and whole melancholy paragraphs carved in sketches in the margins. My dreams are always written down sloppily, in crude half-asleep chicken scratch, nestled between the other entries, marking the space between days. When there are no dreams to mark the space, that in itself becomes a marker that I wasn't paying attention to my dreams.

"Remember that the tattoos on your arms are dark blue stories and your dreams hold the keys to the secret answers of the universe…"
- a old journal entry written by moonlight from me to my future self

The last time I was putting my life back together after it had completely fallen apart I discovered the true power of my journals. When I've been knocked way far off balance it's much easier for me to forget who I am and buy into the idea that everything I've done with my life or cared about in the end just makes me a criminal and a worthless deadbeat with no job skills or diploma that is destined to end up in prison or living on his poor mom's couch forever. My thoughts become plagued with oceans of "if only's" and I wish desperately for another chance to go back and change my sorry fate. When i rediscovered my journals THIS TIME I realized I'd left so many notes for myself from all the other times I went through this and that I already knew myself better than anyone: "Just in case you forgot—things were really bad back here but you pulled through like a champ —you're gonna make it kid." and "don't you ever forget what the sunset looks like from the open door of this boxcar, don't you ever ever forget how alive you are right now. it's still all in you, remember?"

Reading my old journals feels like I'm traveling through time. I suddenly have the ability to revisit earlier lives—but through the eyes of someone older, who sees things from a wiser place. And although I'm obviously the one who wrote them, it's amazing what a different person I feel like now. It's so hard to believe that all those lives were lived by the same person, and that person is me. I wonder what would happen to all those memories if I didn't write them down—if all the ridiculous and dangerous things I've ever done, all the dismal and wondrous places I've ever been, and all the brilliant and revolutionary people I've ever known, weren't documented for me to rediscover like buried treasure lessons in the future. I wonder if all those memories would eventually just dissolve, unnoticed, like tears in rain.

This is my history. This is how I know I've been alive and that I'm not just living with a bunch of somebody else's memories that I watched on television or saw in a movie or read about in the paper. I take notes. And my notes become stories, my stories become lessons, and my lessons become incorporated into my own personal mythology that I carry around with me everywhere. This is what gives the crazy patterns of my life meaning. This is how I map my world.

I hope this book of ours inspires you to make maps of your own.

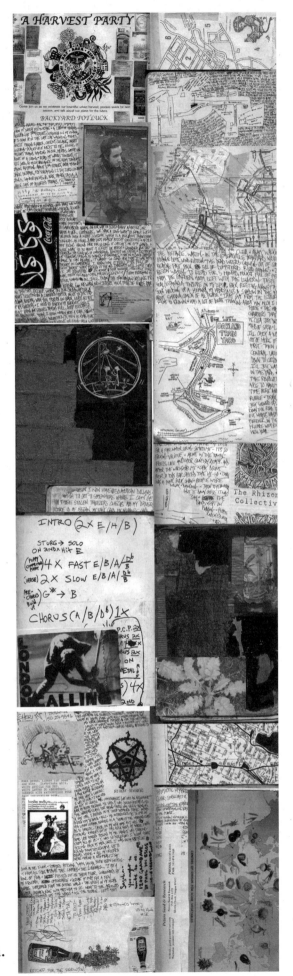

THE BIPOLAR WORLD

First Printed in the
SF Bay Guardian
September 2002
By: Sascha Altman DuBrul

I.

I WAS 18 years old the first time they locked me up in a psych ward. The police found me walking on the subway tracks in New York City, and I was convinced the world was about to end and I was being broadcast live on prime-time TV on all the channels. I hadn't slept for months, and I thought there were microscopic transmitters under my skin that were making me itch and recording everything I was saying for some top-secret branch of the CIA. After I'd walked the tracks through three stations, the cops wrestled me to the ground, arrested me, and brought me to an underground jail cell and then to the emergency room of Bellevue psychiatric hospital, where they strapped me to a bed. Once they managed to track down my terrified mother, she signed some papers, a nurse shot me up with some hardcore antipsychotic drugs, and I woke up two weeks later in the "quiet room" of a public mental hospital upstate.

I'd spent the previous year as a freshman at a prestigious private college in Portland, Or. At some point in the spring, around finals time, I'd gotten sick and gone to the campus health clinic. The school nurse gave me a prescription for penicillin, and I had an allergic reaction to it and almost died. To counteract the effects of the antibiotic, the hospital gave me a hardcore steroid called Prednisone, which totally messed up my sleeping schedule.

But somehow, instead of being tired, I managed to have an infinite amount of energy: I'd ride my bike really fast everywhere and do tons of sit-ups and push-ups after sleeping badly for two hours. Without realizing what was happening, I slipped into a perpetually manic state, talking a mile a minute and juggling a dozen projects that had nothing to do with my schoolwork. I seemed to have a new idea every couple of hours and would lie in bed unable to sleep while the thoughts shot back and forth around my head like a pinball game as I planned out the next 40 years of my life.

At some point I started to think the radio was talking to me, and I started reading all these really deep meanings in the billboards downtown and on the highways that no one else was seeing. I was convinced there were subliminal messages everywhere trying to tell a small amount of people that the world was about to go through drastic changes and we needed to be ready for it. People would talk to me and I was obsessed with the idea that there was this whole other language underneath what we thought we were saying that everyone was using without even realizing it.

My freaked-out friends called my mom, she bought me a plane ticket over the phone, and they somehow managed to get me on a flight back east. When I arrived at the airport with a mind speeding in sixth gear on a dozen different degenerating levels simultaneously, my mom was there to pick me up and bring me back to her apartment on the Upper West Side of Manhattan. I remember her telling me that in the morning she was going to take me to see "a man that could help me." I didn't much like the sound of that; it was obvious that they'd brainwashed her memory clean so that she wouldn't remember what an important role she was playing in the grand scheme, and I had to get out of there.

After I'd been in the psych ward for a while, the doctors diagnosed me with something called bipolar disorder (otherwise known as manic depression) and gave me a mood-stabilizing drug called Depakote. They told my mom to get used to the idea that I had a serious mental disorder I was going to be grappling with for the rest of my life and that I was going to require daily doses of all those medications to be able to function healthily in the outside world.

I didn't realize it at the time, but I, like millions of other Americans, would spend years wrestling with the implications of that diagnosis. Manic depression kills tens of thousands of people, mostly young people, every year. Statistically, one out of every five people diagnosed with the disease eventually commits suicide. But I wasn't convinced, to say the least, that gulping down a handful of pills every day would make me sane.

You have to understand this part of the story: I was raised by parents with pretty radical leftist politics who taught me to question everything and always be skeptical of big business and capitalism. I spent my teenage years growing up in a punk scene that glorified craziness and disrespect for authority. Also, from the time I was a little kid, everyone always said that I was very sensitive to the world around me and to the suffering of others, maybe too sensitive, and I just chalked it up to that. My worldview didn't leave any room for the possibility that my instability and volatility might actually have something to do with biology

When I was 24, I ended up back in the same program, out in the New York suburbs, that my mom had put me in as a teenager. I was miserable and lonely. The doctors weren't quite sure what I had, so they diagnosed me with something called schizoaffective disorder. They gave me an antidepressant called Celexa and an atypical antipsychotic called Zyprexa. I was in group therapy every day. There was an organic farm to work on down the road from the halfway house, and after a couple weeks they let me volunteer there a few hours a day sowing seeds and potting plants in the greenhouse. Eventually I convinced them to let me live there, and I moved out of the halfway house and came for outpatient care just a couple of times a week.

It took a few months, but for the first time I could see that the drugs were actually working for me. It was more than the circumstances; it actually felt chemical. Slowly all the horrible noise and thoughts faded and I started to feel good again. I remember watching an early summer sunset over the fields at the farm and realizing I was happy for the first time in months and months. Once I moved onto the farm full time, I would come into the city on the weekends to work at the farmers market and hang out with my friends. As obvious as it was that the drugs were helping me, I really just saw them as a temporary solution. They made me gain a bunch of weight. I always had a hard time waking up in the morning. My mouth was always dry. They were relatively new drugs, and not even the doctors knew about the long-term side effects of taking them. Besides which, the whole idea just made me feel really uncomfortable. How would I talk to my friends about it? What if there were some global economic crisis and instead of running around with my crew torching banks and tearing up the concrete I was withdrawing from some drug I suddenly didn't have access to anymore? I didn't want to be dependent on the drugs of the Man.

The police picked me up wandering the streets of Los Angeles on New Year's Day 2001. I'd been smashing church windows with my bare fists and running through traffic scaring the hell out of people screaming the lyrics to punk songs, convinced that the world had ended and I was the center of the universe. They locked me up in the psych unit of the L.A. County Jail, and that's where I spent the next month, talking to the flickering fluorescent lightbulbs and waiting for my friends to come break me out.

I was quickly given the diagnosis of bipolar disorder again and loaded down with meds. "That's so reductionistic, so typical of Western science to isolate everything into such simplistic bifurcated relationships," I'd tell the overworked white-coated psychiatrist staring blankly from the other side of the tiny jail cell as I paced back and forth and he scribbled notes on a clipboard that said "Risperdal" in big letters at the top. "If anything I'm multi-polar, poly-polar I go to poles you'd never even be able to dream up in your imaginationless science or with all those drugs you're shooting me up with. You're all a bunch of fools!" And so I paced my cell.

Finally after the month in jail, a couple of weeks in a Kaiser psych ward, and four months in a halfway house for people with severe psychiatric disabilities, I got it together enough to be able to move back into my old collective house in North Oakland. I was taking a mood-stabilizing drug called lithium and an antidepressant called Wellbutrin.

And that's when I finally started doing the research I'd been putting off for so long. After a year of not being able to read, I started to pick up some books I'd collected about manic depression. And that's when I really began the internal and external dialogue about my condition, when I began to put the puzzle together and to make sense of it all so it wasn't just a bunch of isolated pieces that didn't fit together. I started talking to friends really openly and using the column I had in a punk rock magazine as a forum to talk about madness and manic depression. And I started coming to terms with the paradox that, however much contempt I feel toward the pharmaceutical industry for making a profit from manic-depressive people's misery and however much I aspire to be living outside the system, the drugs help keep me alive, and in the end I'm so thankful for them.

II.

The Aug. 19, 2002, issue of Time states that 2.3 million people in the United States suffer from bipolar disorder. Given the vast number of people BPD affects on a daily basis, I'm amazed by how few books there are on the subject. Considering that young folks are the most heavily affected part of the population, the lack of books written about them seems particularly striking.

The Time article states that the average age of onset for BPD has fallen in a single generation from the early 30s to the late teens. And while it's unclear whether those stats have more to do with the current diagnostic procedures or some other societal variable, the fact is that BPD characteristically hits folks for the first time as teenagers.

It's confusing enough being a teenager in a society that's obviously so twisted and manic itself. Imagine being told to swallow that (a) you're the one who's sick, not the society; and (b) it's the society's medicine that is going to cure you. A hard sell for sure. It partly explains the high stats of psych-med noncompliance and high average of readmittance to hospitals long after initial diagnosis. So where are the books for teens?

When I was institutionalized as a teenager in the early 1990s, the book the doctors recommended to my mom was called A Brilliant Madness: Living with Manic Depressive Illness, by Patty Duke and Gloria Hochman. This was the standard reading at the time, the book that all the doctors recommended if a family member had been diagnosed with BPD. A movie star before my generation's time, Duke describes in her memoir a rocky passage from childhood to suburban motherhood (with two children of her own) and all of her traumatic swings between mania and depression until she discovered lithium and finally got her life under control. Her story from disaster to eventual recovery and success, mixed with musings about the nature of the illness, are interspersed with more technical chapters using case studies by Hochman, a medical reporter.

Going back and reading this book a decade after its first publication, I was definitely more impressed with it than I remember being as a teenager. Although it reads less like a piece of literature and more like the self-help book that it is, A Brilliant Madness stands as the first popular book of its time to really talk about the nature and treatment of manic depression. Unfortunately, to a skeptical 21st-century teen diagnosed with BPD, I think it would leave a lot to be desired.

Eight years later, when I was pacing my cell in the L.A. County Jail and being given shots of Haldol to keep me from setting off the sprinkler system, the book the doctors recommended to my mom was An Unquiet Mind: A Memoir of Moods and Madness, by Dr. Kay Redfield Jamison. First published in 1995, in recent years it has become the book everyone reads about manic depression. Jamison is an interesting one: not only is she a psychiatrist but she's also bipolar herself and has been through the suicidally depressed and delusionally manic mood swings like the most dramatic and tormented of us. She also has quite a flair for writing, with a poetic command of language that left me smiling and reading certain passages over and over again. I would venture to guess that not too many psychiatrists out there use great words like "mercurial," "cauldronous," and "glacially." I found the book well thought-out and beautifully written.

Jamison has another, less well-known book called <u>Touched with Fire: Manic Depressive Illness and the Artistic Temperament</u>. While more academic and dense, the book attempts to draw out the connection between creative genius and bipolar disorder, using as examples such classic artists and writers as Virginia Woolf, T.S. Eliot, Hermann Hesse, Vincent van Gogh, and Jackson Pollock. I finished the book with the new understanding that I'm a part of a group of people that has been misunderstood and persecuted throughout history, but meanwhile has been responsible for some of the most brilliant of history's creations. I found the book rewarding in its attempts to tackle difficult questions about the nature of lithium treatment and the price artists pay in deciding whether to take the drugs. And questions about what would happen if people like us were actually weeded out through future genetic technology.

<u>Touched with Fire</u> left me wondering what a book about the relationship between bipolar disorder and creativity would look like if it was a little less academic and if the examples used were more contemporary artists and musicians, people whom (less classically cultured) folks from my generation might have actually heard of and be able to relate to.

 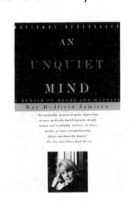 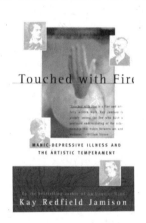  

III.

At the beginning of this past summer, it seemed my question was partly solved. A friend brought to my attention a new book titled <u>Detour: My Bipolar Road Trip in 4-D</u> by a young woman named Lizzie Simon who was definitely thinking along similar lines. Diagnosed bipolar when she was 17 and now a successful theater producer in New York City with the help of her daily dose of lithium, Simon decided to travel across the country and interview other "successful" people who were bipolar and write about her adventures along the way. I was excited that, at long last, there was finally a book written by a person about my age dealing with our affliction. It's a quick read, definitely more my generation's speed, with short chapters that draw the reader in and a racy love story thrown in for good measure. And although I felt like I could connect to it on some levels, I still found something lacking.

Both Jamison's <u>Unquiet Mind</u> and Simon's <u>Detour</u> begin by talking about how idyllic and wonderful the authors' childhoods were. I think in both instances they're trying to drive home the point that their problems really are genetic in origin, that bipolar disorder can strike in the nicest of homes. But honestly, I just had a hard time relating to their good fortune. While I found

Simon's descriptions of teenage mania eerily similar to my own stories and felt a connection in her enthusiasm and her drive to reach out to others like herself, her lack of consciousness about her own economic privilege in relation to the rest of the world smacked of the naivete of someone who's never stepped outside of the bubble of her upper class.

I kept thinking: If I'm having a hard time relating to this and I grew up relatively upper-middle-class, what about all the kids who read my column and send me letters who come from really dysfunctional working-class families? Who can they look to for inspiration and support?

And I found myself asking still deeper questions that no one else around me seemed to be able to answer: How do these drugs I'm taking actually work? What effects are they having on my brain chemistry? What's actually going on up there as I swing back and forth between mania and depression? As a college dropout with no background in molecular biology, neurology, or anything close to it, I started working my way through Essential Psychopharmacology: Neuroscientific Basis and Practical Applications, by Stephen M. Stahl, which was recommended to me by my psychiatrist at Kaiser as the most clear and well-written psych-med textbook available.

Reading it, I felt strangely like one of the androids in the 1980s sci-fi movie *Blade Runner*, the one about the droids who are so smart they've found their own blueprints and have gone looking desperately for their creator to help them reprogram themselves for longer life just before their time is up. Here I was, 27 years old, grappling with the intense reality that I have a genetic mental disease that supposedly only gets worse with age, lying in bed at night studying these complex diagrams in a psychopharmacology textbook, very conscious of the fact that my brain was reading about itself, that I was reading my own blueprints.

In the end, what it comes down to for me is that I desperately feel the need to connect with other folks like myself so I can validate my experiences and not feel so damn alone in the world, so I can pass along the lessons I've learned to help make it easier for other people struggling like myself. By my nature and the way I was raised, I don't trust mainstream medicine or corporate culture, but the fact that I'm sitting here writing this essay right now is proof that their drugs are helping me. And I'm looking for others out there with similar experiences.

But I feel so alienated sometimes, even by the language I find coming out of my mouth or that I type out on the computer screen. Words like "disorder," "disease," and "dysfunction" just seem so very hollow and crude. I feel like I'm speaking a foreign and clinical language that is useful for navigating my way though the current system but doesn't translate into my own internal vocabulary, where things are so much more fluid and complex. Toward the end of An Unquiet Mind, Jamison points out that even the term "bipolar" seems to obscure and minimize the illness it is supposed to represent by presupposing a polarization between two states that aren't always so easily picked apart. But "bipolar" seems to be the word we're stuck with for the moment.

Our society still seems to be in the early stages of the dialogue where you're either "for" or "against" the mental health system. Like either you swallow the antidepressant ads on television as modern-day gospel and start giving your dog Prozac, or you're convinced we're living in Brave New World and all the psych drugs are just part of a big conspiracy to keep us from being self-reliant and realizing our true potential. I think it's really about time we start carving some more of the middle ground with stories from outside the mainstream and creating a new language for ourselves that reflects all the complexity and brilliance that we hold inside.

crazy

by Kika Kat

it had been kind of a rough in spring in olympia and I really wanted to go away for awhile, to sort it all out in my head. ariel was driving up to one of the northern gulf islands, so when she offered to loan me her bike and her buckets and maegan and I a ride to a place where we could begin a bike trip, and when maegan began giving me detailed reports of her island research, it wasn't too hard to say yes. ariel was going to pick us up at the ferry on her way back down.

a couple days into the trip maegan and I biked to an island preserve, a place that was supposed to be magical and calm, full of tide pools, birds, and large trees. for a while we sat on the rocks together in silence, and then maegan went for a walk. I stayed, looking out over the sea, and suddenly my mind began fogging over. it was that terrible feeling, familiar and overwhelming and awful. I started feeling scared, out of control, like I could do anything right then, not the good things like flying but the bad things like getting lost on those awful, well marked path trails, or throwing myself down onto the rocks below me, or going crazy and not coming back. crazy still scares me sometimes, even though I've been working with it for so long. even though my friend gunner assures me that in fact i am crazy, but that it's only my fear of it that makes me so miserable.

i've gone through the cycles so many times. i've planned out every suicide so that in case it doesn't end sometime, in case it doesn't leave of its own accord, i'll still have a way out. but it makes me sad, these days, to have that kind of backup plan, because i really want to live. and i guess that's the problem, i guess if i was willing to settle for being alive but mitigated or medicated, i might not be so extreme, it might not be so dramatically all or nothing.

i don't know what the swings are actually called; i've never been tested for anything or had any diagnosis other than the concern of people who love me. mania, bi-polarity; panic disorder, schizophrenia; words get tossed around too freely and make boxes too quickly. whatever it is it's a big part of my struggle, a struggle that has to be taken in context: a young white american woman alive on a dying planet, a citizen in the place most responsible for modern death and destruction. is slight schizophrenia the natural response to holding two worlds in one body? there is the world that i come from, a construct of human creations, an elaborate labyrinth of manufactured distraction which, due to my globally unique position of privilege, will comfort me as the planet goes down, will gently turn my head away from the gore and close a silencing door between it and me, and offer me a latte. and then there is the world that i am made of, a world of sticks and stones and breaking bones, a wild world i am terribly estranged from. a world i remember and long for but which is separated from me by a gap grown wide from too many generations of not speaking that language. it's a painful dichotomy, a tortuous one. to know home but have no way back and no way forward. to be locked out forever. to know there was only one key and we smelt it down to make coke cans and cars. it's insane, the dichotomy. the dichotomy is crazy.

when i'm solid i'm so solid. when i'm good i'm very very good. but i can't count on myself to stay stable. new friends get hurt, confused, annoyed; old friends eventually lose patience. a shiny few see the heart of me and believe in it. and hold my hand when i'm down and hold my place when i'm up, and they're the ones who get my gifts, just because they see it that way. because they want what i actually have. it's rare and exhilarating to give someone just what they need, without calculating. to be just the right medicine, as you are, so you can finally be generous. to find a place where your nature is asked to be nothing but true and the exacting weight of expectations that you never chose for yourself is lifted.

a place where you are free and honest about the instability that exists inside you, instead of trying to cover it up or hold it together. trying and trying and always failing that false goal.

MAKING SENSE OF BEING CALLED CRAZY IN A CRAZY WORLD...

WHAT IS NORMAL?

Who gets to decide? Politicians? CEOs? Principals? Doctors?

What does it mean to be called "mentally ill" in a world that is obviously mad?

The definition of mental illness is relative to the culture drawing the boundaries. And it certainly seems that modern society has gone over the edge.

We live in a culture where it's considered healthy to eat food made out of toxic chemicals and happiness is defined as something that can't hurt you, like steady jobs and gated communities. We live in a society where affluent people prevent wrinkles by paralyzing their facial muscles with bacteria and prevent worry by implanting computer chips in the bodies of their pets. We live in a country that has more prison inmates than farmers. We live in a world where McDonalds was allowed to build a restaurant in front of the pyramids in Egypt. We live in times where it is normal to believe *Good Morning America* and considered radical to ever think that people like doctors and reporters might not always be telling the truth.

Are we delusional and dysfunctional, or is it the culture we live in?

"...The first time I was hospitalized I asked a night duty nurse why I was there. 'Because you have a mania,' she replied. 'How is my mania on insisting that the world is an irrational place any different from your mania on insisting that the world is rational?' The nurse turned and walked off, probably to scrawl 'delusions of grandeur' on my record...." – B.F.

When your brain is the one breaking down, the idea of mental illness seems **excruciatingly real.**

When you start to ask the authorities questions like

What are Mental Illnesses?

you tend to get answers like:

These answers reassure a lot of people. They make it clear mental illness isn't a result of weakness. They take away a lot of the shame. And they offer a hope that mental illness can be treated with drugs and standard medical procedure, like any other disease.

In general, they're disorders of the brain, your body's most important organ.

A mental illness is:
- a health condition, much like heart disease or diabetes
- no one's fault -- not the person's, nor the family's.

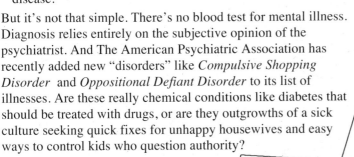

But it's not that simple. There's no blood test for mental illness. Diagnosis relies entirely on the subjective opinion of the psychiatrist. And The American Psychiatric Association has recently added new "disorders" like *Compulsive Shopping Disorder* and *Oppositional Defiant Disorder* to its list of illnesses. Are these really chemical conditions like diabetes that should be treated with drugs, or are they outgrowths of a sick culture seeking quick fixes for unhappy housewives and easy ways to control kids who question authority?

When you ask some people

What are mental illnesses?

you get answers like:

"Mental illness" is a convenient label for behavior that disrupts the social order.

You get answers like: people who notice how screwed up the world is, or who perceive reality in radically different ways than "normal" folks, and then display "extreme" reactions, get labeled with a disease. Which could render dumpster-diving and Christian fundamentalism a form of pathology, depending on who's making the diagnosis. Consider: a kid can't sit still in class and wants to talk when he has an idea, instead of when he gets called on. Is the kid out of control and in need of Ritalin, or is it possible that school is actually incredibly regimented, unimaginative, and mind-numbing to the point that a child with an active, inquisitive brain might find it very difficult to pay attention? According to the DSM-IV, the official diagnostic manual of the American Psychiatric Association, a behavior "clinically significant" enough to be labeled a disorder must not be "an expectable and culturally sanctioned response to a particular event." So if an average American responds to any given atrocity—like the fact that people are starving in countries all over the world where farmers are being forced to grow coffee for America instead of food for their people—with an expectable and culturally sanctioned response, like turning on the television to avoid thinking about it, they are healthy. Whereas if I sob hysterically and talk to strangers about it and stay up all night trying to think of ways to change it, I might be the one who gets labeled with a disorder.

But you can't stay up all night every night. The world is full of atrocities.
If you can't filter some of them out you are going to explode.

How do you know if you have a problem?

t h e r e   i s   n o   o n e   a n s w e r

Except this: it depends who you're asking.

> **What does it mean *to you* to be functional?**

The DSM-IV stresses a "marked impairment in occupational functioning." When the World Bank was trying to find a way to gauge the cost of mental illness, they came up with the measurement *days out of role*. As in the number of days a person is unable to perform the role expected of them: stockbroker, mother, factory worker, full-time student.

On one hand this makes some sense. Everyone gets down, right? If you can keep your problems in your head you're doing all right, but if they really get in the way of functioning **where it counts**—school or work—then it's time to worry, right?

But what if you never wanted to perform one of these roles?

They will assure you and your family with statements like:

Are you, your family, and your doctors aiming for the same version of healthy? What does mental health look like to you?

Mental illnesses are treatable.
With proper treatment, many people with a mental illness get well and lead productive lives.

"Mental Health Seen As Ultimate Productivity Weapon
Rise of Mental Disorders Becoming Major Business Issue"
(Actual title of the keynote paper for World Mental Health Day 2000, sponsored by the World Mental Health Foundation)

According to the author of this study, Bill Wilkerson, we are seeing "a deepening dependence of global corporations on the minds rather than the backs and muscles of those who work for them. Mental capacity will do the 'heavy lifting' in the information economy. The mental capacity to do productive work is under unprecedented attack from a complicated network of social, economic, biological and genetic forces. 'An impenetrable maze' as Harvard researchers have called it. The stage is thus set for a global business agenda on mental health starting with the proposition that mental health is an important business productivity weapon in an intensely competitive data-based world economy."

Do you want to regain your mental capacity so you can do some "heavy lifting" or so you can live out the role you've chosen for yourself as fully as possible? How do you trust the people who are supposed to help you when they're part of this same system?

"WHAT GETS ME IS THAT SHOPPING, AS WE ALL REMEMBER, WAS THE NATIONALLY PRESCRIBED MEDICATION FOR THE NATIONAL DEPRESSION AFTER 9/11."-eduardo

You can't always trust the authorities to know what's best.

who is telling your doctor what to think?

Timothy Kelly (aka Madliberator to Icarus Project folk) published a few salient observations on the links between the psychiatric profession and the pharmaceutical industry in a recent communique from Clamor magazine:

Is giving people drugs so they can function as normal in a pathological world equivalent to genetically engineering plants to grow in damaged soil?

same

"I remember being shocked by the amount of pharmaceutical advertisement in my psychiatrist's office. Pens, notebooks, a thermos, and even a clock all proudly displayed the name of products like Paxil, Prozac, and Zyprexa. On the coffee table a stack of magazines published by drug companies were filled with full color glossy advertisements of drugs. It occurred to me that this advertisement was not directed at me, the patient, but at my doctor.

The pharmaceutical industry spends over 15 billion dollars annually on advertising, and roughly a quarter of their total profits come from the sale of psychiatric medication, more than any other disease or ailment (*Boston Globe*, 5/8/02). The American Psychiatric Association receives much of its funding, including for research, from pharmaceutical companies. **Essentially, we have an extremely lucrative industry exerting huge financial influence over the medical field, particularly psychiatry, an area ripe for profit due to the fact that it's not burdened by the same expectations of biological proof as other areas of medicine.**

At one time, the state relied on religious authority to justify sanctions on thought and behavior. Nowadays this authority has been transferred to Psychiatrists in the name of science. Burning people at the stake as heretics gave way to frontal lobotomies for schizophrenics;

"WHATEVER DEFINITION OF **NORMAL** IS USED, THE FACT IS THAT THIS TYPE OF BEHAVIOR -- WHAT IS CALLED NORMAL -- IS IN ITSELF ONE OF THE MOST DANGEROUS FORMS OF BEHAVIOR EVER SEEN ON EARTH. THE OBEDIENCE, THE CONSUMPTION, THE UNQUESTIONING APPROACH, THE VIOLENCE..." –DAVID OAKS

DOCTORS HELP A LOT OF PEOPLE.

lobotomies have given way to tranquilizers and "quiet rooms." (So, yes, the level of violence has decreased from murder to surgery, from surgery to drugs and captivity.) Still, the underlying purpose of the violence, whether the authority is derived from science or religion, remains the same: social hygiene and control."

MEDICINE HELPS A LOT OF PEOPLE.

We live in an imperfect world.
Do what you have to do to survive.

THEY _DO_ SAVE LIVES.

Think for yourself.

19

TOO CLOSE TO THE SUN

a really sad story about my dead friend who was manic-depressive like me   by sascha

I was at my house in Oakland when the phone call came. A mutual friend in the Mid-West who heard from her friend in Oregon about a girl back on the East Coast who jumped off a bridge. She thought it might just be a rumor. I didn't believe it and that's what I said: "Naw man, I just talked to Sera a week ago -- she was going traveling and had a ticket to Europe in February. She said she had been a little down but she didn't sound so bad. She always goes through her waves of depression like the rest of us." But my heart was beating fast and my fingers were starting to shake.

"It's true man, she's dead. I'm sorry to have to be the one to tell you. Things have been really strange around here the last couple days." That was Spam in West Philadelphia. I had called his house after talking to Sera's voicemail. "Everyone around here is freaking out. You two were really close, huh? I'm really sorry." Shock. Disbelief. As the tears started falling down my face I could suddenly feel this unfamiliar emotion rising up inside of me the same way that you can sometimes feel unfamiliar muscles in your body the day after doing a new exercise. And it hurt. It really hurt.

Sera and I had a lot in common. We were both hopeless romantics and suffered from crazy wanderlust. We waxed poetic over freight trains and the call of the open road. Sera and I ended up hitchhiking all the way across the country to go to those historic protests against the World Trade Organization in Seattle and we had mad adventures all along the way. We were never satisfied with our work -- no matter how much we were doing. We both threw ourselves into crazy situations just to feel alive -- just to feel things really intensely. We were both running from the ghosts of our childhoods and found our peace out on the open road -- in the excitement of the new, the stories of strangers, and in the struggle for justice.

We were also both manic depressive.

One of our big conflicts while we were traveling was that she was always trying to get me to stop taking my psych drugs. She said that they slowed me down. The whole idea of them just made her uncomfortable. Sera didn't believe in a life without extremes and she didn't want her experiences mediated by some drug made by The Man. They just want you to think that you can't take care of yourself without those drugs, she'd say. She'd taken Prozac for a while when she was a teenager and had hated it. It made her numb. It killed her sex drive. She said she just couldn't feel anything real when she was on it. She got off it quick and didn't look back.

As for so many of us, psych drugs symbolized defeat in Sera's eyes. Like having to spend your last money on a greyhound after getting kicked out of the trainyard and the highway. But worse because it means so much more than popping a couple pills: taking psych meds seems to mean adopting a completely different lifestyle. It means having health insurance so it means having a job so it means staying in one place so it means being stable, a worker bee. The pills are a constant reminder that you're dependent on the system that you hate to keep you alive and healthy—you're tied right into the death machine.

And doesn't everybody have mood swings? At what point does it become something that gets the label "disease?" At what point, if any, does it make sense to start taking the drugs? So many of my friends could probably be diagnosed as some form of "crazy" by mainstream psychiatrists because a lot of mainstream psychiatrists are just like pawns of the big drug companies (which are in fact very evil and just want to dole out as much product as they can and get you hooked so you'll always be coming back for the fix.) As a subculture we don't usually take the whole "crazy" thing too seriously. It's a word that me and my people throw around with ease.

But the reality is that a lot of us struggle with our own madness and we don't always find ways of coping that work. There is a point where you have to draw the line and come to some kind of conclusion about the nature of your problems. To give you an example from my own life:

This time last year I was sitting in a tiny cell in the psych unit of Los Angeles County Jail convinced that the world as we had known it had just ended and we were all living on in dreamtime and that everyone I saw was just a reflection of me so it didn't matter what I did. In short, by all measurements, I was totally stark raving loony toons.

What happened wasn't inevitable. I'd stopped taking my psych drugs a few month earlier because it seemed obvious that I didn't need them anymore and I was just being my usual hectic self: working on too many projects, leaving piles of paper everywhere, riding around on my bike and being super busy.

Then at some point things began to get a little out of control. I stopped sleeping well at night because my head was constantly bursting with amazing ideas. My thoughts started to get more desperate. Everything started to seem very relevant. I mean everything. My mind suddenly had the power to take any two things and draw connections between them. The projects I was working on suddenly seemed very very important, even urgent. I felt like I had discovered THE secret that was going to bring everyone together -- unite everyone in the world against the global power structure. I was reading a book called Revolutionary Suicide by Huey P. Newton and books about COINTELPRO, the program the FBI used to destabilize activist groups in the '70's. I started getting paranoid. I started to have the very disconcerting feeling that I was about to die, that there were important people that wanted me dead.

I stopped hanging out with anyone who knew me well and I started hanging out with people who had just met me and didn't find it so disturbing that I had slipped totally off my rocker. I started walking up to total strangers on the street and talking to them and have amazing conversations. I'd walk to the community garden down the street and just hang with the plants. I was so in tune with the universe that I could feel every last blade of grass as if they were breathing with me. Each plant had an incredibly different personality and I would spend hours just listening to them talk to me. It was so incredible. Meanwhile, I began to get more and more estranged from my community. My housemates were scared of me. Everyone was talking about me behind my back, but no one had the courage to actually confront me.

At some point my mom came out to visit from New York and in her typical fashion, proceeded to organize a bunch of my friends together to take some direct action. One night they sat me down and pleaded with me to start taking my drugs again. I was furious.

Were they fucking blind? Hadn't they been reading the news? Didn't they realize that the pharmaceutical companies and the agro-chemical companies had merged into the LIFE SCIENCE INDUSTRY and these people wanted nothing less than enslavement of the human race and control of the entire planet? These were the same people who were trying to genetically engineer the world's crops to be dependent on their herbicides, the same ones who created the technology that can make seed crops reproduce sterile. It's so American to think that you can fix everything with a pill or feed people with chemicals. Hadn't they read Huxley's Brave New World? How could they not see what was going on when it was so obviously right in front of their eyes? You want me to trust these people's medicine? You gotta be kidding me. These people peddle pesticides to farmers in the developing world and graft human ears to lab mice. They are evil motherfuckers. I'm not going to put those drugs in my body -- they're just going to kill the parts of my brain that are working so well! You just want me to be a robot like the rest of you. Fuck that shit and fuck all of you!

And so off to Los Angeles I went, to get myself locked up in jail. I've been told that it's very hard to argue with someone who is not only manic and delusional but not really that far off the mark. For brevity's sake I'll spare all the details, but let me just say that I'm very lucky I didn't end up with an LAPD bullet in my chest.

They say that most manic-depressives go off their drugs a bunch of times before they either kill themselves or realize that they need them. That's a hard one to hear, and I still don't completely believe it, but mania is alluring for sure. They say that we get addicted to the intensity like a drug.

But of course the problem with the intensity is that it's like a pendulum swing -- if you swing too far over to one side, you're inevitably going to swing back over in the other direction. I can plot the last eight years of my life on a graph and it would look like a big sine wave. Huge peaks and dips. And the upswings have been responsible for everything cool I've ever done in my life. But the downs are miserable.

I can't really get mad at Sera. She wasn't in control of herself when she jumped off that bridge. She just wanted the pain to end. She just felt so uncomfortable in her own skin that she couldn't take it anymore. Suicide is not a malicious act. I spent four months of last year totally suicidal and psychotic, stuck in a miserable halfway house for people with severe psychiatric disabilities, far away from all my friends, my head eating itself alive with self-hatred and despair. Manic-depression is a sickness, a disease. But it's more complicated because it always seems like it's the most brilliant and talented people like Sera who are cursed with it. It's a blessing and a curse -- an imbalance of chemicals in their brains that torments them but lets them see and feel things other people can't; allows them to create art and music and words that grab people by the heart and soul -- allows them to kiss the sky and come back down to tell the tale.

In the interests of sticking around the planet for a while, I'm learning new dances with the enemy. At least for now I've made my choice to take the drugs and deal with all the sacrifices that go along with that choice: not being able to stay up all night, slowing down, staying in one place, holding down a job for more than a couple months at a time, going to a bunch of therapy, all things I've always been so scared of. But I really really want to live and I really want to grapple with my demons and I know it's going to take a long time. I was really worried the drugs were going to turn me into a zombie, but trust me: I feel strong emotions everyday, I need something to keep that shit in check. This isn't exactly the path I pictured myself walking down, but here I am, walking it.

And Sera's not. It's so hard to believe she's dead. Sera had such wide open traveler eyes. I can't help but remember little things like how when we were on the road we'd wake up in the morning and tell each other our dreams. She taught me this word once in Armenian: yavroos, which translated to something like "one who knows your soul." I loved that woman something real. She bared her soul to me. She still feels so alive. And that's the strange paradox about the whole thing: I think it's really because that she really was more alive than most of us. She felt things more, she took more risks, she refused to play by society's rules, she lived with an intensity that most people only ever dream of -- she lived her life like someone who always felt like she didn't have enough time. She lived fast and died young just like she figured she was going to. She wrote hundreds of pages that are inevitably going to be published and change a whole lot of people's lives. She's leaving her mark for sure.

But it's really sad and I can't stop thinking of that ancient Greek myth of Icarus and his wings of wax. In the old story, Icarus' father Daedalus builds a pair of wings out of wax and feathers for his son so that they can escape from the island they've been imprisoned on. Despite all his father's warnings, Icarus flies too close to the sun, melts his beautiful wings, and falls into the ocean to his death. The moral of the story being that Icarus was fortunate enough to have been given wings, but he wasn't patient enough to learn how to stay balanced -- he couldn't see anything but soaring as high as he could, so he ended up in the sea.

I wanted to get old with Sera Bilizikian still in my life. I just figured that that's the way it would be. I just want her back now and it's not going to happen. Sera had a beautiful pair of wings that carried her to faraway places and on amazing journeys. She burned bright in her short twenty-three years, did a lot of good for the world while she was here, and will be missed by many many people. I hope that as a community we can learn the lessons from this horrible tragedy, and that it inspires us to learn how to understand and take better care of each other.

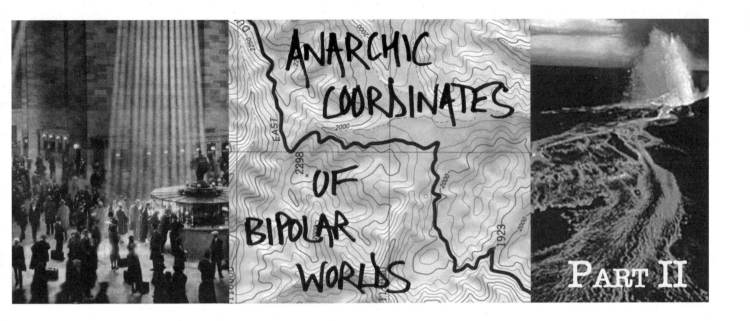

ANARCHIC COORDINATES OF BIPOLAR WORLDS

PART II

In these pages we've tried to put together some of the complex and jagged pieces of our experiences to give you a sense from the inside of what it's like to live with this thing they call bipolar disorder.

Mania, Depression, and the Territory Between

In an attempt to find language that can map the extremes of our landscapes, we've drawn the following paragraphs from letters we've received and the words people have posted on The Icarus Project website, interspersed with our own commentary (*in italics*).

One of the first things we've noticed is that there seems to be a universal wave function underlying bipolar experience; like a pendulum, our moods and subsequently the course of our lives, will swing down as far as they swing up, and the two extremes can't seem to exist without each other, unless the pendulum comes to equilibrium closer to the center.

"It is as if my thoughts have sailed away. I can see them in the distance, but I can't access them. I feel like I've experienced an amazing dream where everything came together and fit in gorgeous geometrical patterns. And now, my reality crowds around me like stale smoke. I feel cowardly, inept, and worthless." -emiko

Though bipolar affects an astonighingly wide range of people, it seems to give many of us the feeling that we are somehow different in ways other people might not ever notice.

"First of all, I live about the most "normal" life imaginable. I have a husband. I teach school. I have three kids. I go to their ballgames. I go to Church. Even though my life appears to be normal to the person who hardly knows me, I really wonder, "Can someone with BP ever truly be normal?" I can sit in a meeting with all the teachers and ten minutes before they come up with the plan, I have already planned and executed everything in my mind. Sometimes I feel like I am going to have a "meltdown" yet no one around me even knows. With the help of medication, I am maintaining a "look" of normalcy. Yet, I wonder how long it will actually last this time. Do non-BP people even have the remotest idea of the magnitude with which we feel emotion? Is this the curse or the blessing of this disorder?" –bpbear

23

Bipolar seems to mark all of us with an intense sensitivity to the world we live in. So often it becomes too much to handle.

"I remember sitting in a thrift store parking lot, at night in winter Cleveland, staring at the parking lights just thinking of the oil, the people who got the oil, the people who sell the oil, the people who use the oil, and just how insane it all was. It felt like I was the only one who knew that this was all going to have to end, that there wasn't enough and we weren't conserving it. This pretty much drove me crazy. I went from science to self-discovery in an attempt to make sense of it all when I was about 16, started smoking, tripping, all that. I would like to say that it has helped, helped me discover the realm of "more than me" and basically sparked the spiritual side of my life. The only problem is addiction. I've been addicted ever since. I think that it's been my way of medicating the "craziness" and feeling of this world, both good and bad." -ilove

Part of what's so distressing about being manic-depressive is that you feel like you're given access, at times, to brilliant and seemingly secret visions of the world—and when they are snatched away without warning it's so hard to stop chasing after them.

"At times I can find so much meaning in every tiny little thing around that most "normal" people might never throughout their entire life think about twice. Like the flow of a small stream of water after a misty rain or even that first breath of fresh air you inhale after a day or two of not leaving the house because of a manic or depressed episode. At the times in my life when it seems everything is right, when I can find a significance in life, when I'm at peace... those times are what the depression of bipolar disorder destroys in an instant when it hits. Creating a cul-de-sac at almost every road you turn down. Like an endless vicious cycle of deceit played out on another level of thought. Like a chess game that you've mastered through brilliant strategy, and you're about to capture the queen with a silent pawn and in that last pouncing move the board flips and you start over again. Like a Sisyphus cycle of damnation, endlessly rolling that rock to the top only to watch it tumble." -Jereme

Sometimes you build a universe in your mind that is like an intricate house of cards, and though you think it's impenetrable, only a breath or the flick of a fingertip can make it all fall down around you. The pendulum never remains at its highest point; it swings from ecstasy and revelation to suicidal depression according to its own laws of physics.

"I'd spent the first part of that fall flying through uncharted regions of human understanding, convinced that the secret to world peace was the simple fact that the carbon in our bodies was born in the supernovas of huge stars, so we were all obviously the same. This made me ecstatically happy. This was by far the most compelling piece of information on the planet and I was going to share it with every high school student in America. When I failed a biology test, however, the infrastructure of the universe seemed to fall apart. Within a few weeks I was calling Al at the suicide hotline to mutter about how I should obviously either stop existing or move to a beach in Hawaii. All that crap about the stars seemed to be laughing at me." -a

They say that the cycle begins with mania

Mania

In your incendiary seasons you sob with relief, you push late nights through early mornings into the landscapes of raw wonder only visible to eyes which have not closed in sleep for a long time. You stagger and become drunk on beauty, your hands shake, you forget food and feed instead on the light-mad dance of moths flinging themselves against the screen, against the bright bulb of your lamp which burns all day and all night.

by Dalia

You glow and grow, you burn, your eyes shining at stranger and beloved alike until the blur of disappearing distinction renders old categories obsolete and you walk in the street with hands open and trembling.

You leave home more and more often, you find home everywhere you go, and the ones you love are beginning to drag anyway on your wildness and flight.

You love them and you speed on without them, hearing but not heeding their soft drones of worry like bees or flies humming, with a shake of your head you wave them away, truly meaning to listen later.

Anyway all is home and all are family, you flare with ecstasy, tears stream from you as easily as words, you touch with grateful astonishment their warm wet coursing down your face. Inspiration shakes you with its sudden violence as for the first time you see that you will die before you have said a tenth of all that is in you. The hard fisted fact of mortality dogs your heels and you race before it like a flaming leaf in autumn, it's vanishing colors in brilliant last hurrah before the brown dust of November crumbles you once more.

DYNAMITE
To explode
Afraid of
To sit on
To find
To lose
To set off
In auto
To carry
Sticks of

You're not alone in this. Some are drawn mothlike to you and it is your turn now to flame and sputter, loving and illuminating and

burning all you touch.

Some still reach

towards you with singed fingers and smoke filled clothes. Your fuse crackles, you explode in their arms, and some even then hold you still, your burnt rubber smell.

your eyes like   cinders fading fast

There is a moment when the universe seems to expand—we find ourselves with boundless energy and sharpened vision, noticing more and more of the connections between everything in the world around us, and feeling compelled to talk about them constantly. The psychiatric establishment calls this "hypomania," or mild mania, and it is the furthest that some of us reach on our upswings. It is intoxicating. In these early stages we tend to become incredibly confident and magnetic to the people around us, and often find ourselves dreaming up grandiose projects and becoming the center of attention. Sometimes we find ourselves becoming intensely irritable and impatient.

As mania accelerates, it becomes much more urgent to plan and create than it becomes to sleep or take care of ourselves. We are suddenly so much more electric and moving so much faster than everyone else that it seems like our worlds hardly intersect though we are inhabiting the same space. Although we start making less and less sense to the people around us, we see synchronicities everywhere. Everything we experience seems to fit into a master plan of the universe that no one else has access to. At the height of our manias it might seem like we have a direct line to God or simply to the meaning of the universe; we pass through states of intense euphoria and spiritual enlightenment on our way to the Truth. Sometimes it seems like the world is full of nothing but hypocrisy and everyone we love is turning on us, and we become furious, destructive, and full of rage. Sometimes it becomes abundantly clear that the government and/or our personal demons are coming to get us and we are haunted by paranoid certainty of grand conspiracies and imminent apocalypse. One of the biggest challenges for people like us is attempting to make sense afterwards of the visions we have during our manias. In our society it seems our revelations are considered psychosis if we choose to believe there might be any truth in them.

The Beginning of the Cycle. It is hard to know where to draw the line between having boundless energy, seeing meaning everywhere, and behavior that is symptomatic of a problem: budding mania.

"Stopped sleeping much. Waking up early all the time. Had vivid thoughts again. Then one day started seeing illuminated patterns rising up out of the dirt. Found myself hiking through canyons that were suddenly so lucidly cut out of the sky that their immensity became comprehensible and I could see all of them at once. Could see time in the rocks and feel weight in the air. Somehow climbed 3000 feet in 3 miles without feeling like I'd gone anywhere at all. Bounding up switchbacks and intoxicated on sunlight. Ardently discussing the roundness of the moon with god and the sky. Understanding all the ways in which the word mountain is a container for the whole universe. How language gives us stopping points, words like "normal" give us a way to say this is where I end and pathology begins, demarcate chunks of the universe and keep them separate, how language gives us ways to categorize all of our behavior as ok or not ok, to begin censoring ourselves with their words for the experiences that feel inseparable from our souls...
Was I becoming manic? Is that what I have to call this? Or was I having a "true" experience? Was I closer to god or crazy?"
-icarus

At some point the insights and theories evolving in our brains become so all-consuming that we feel an urgent need to communicate them to everyone… We talk too much and become irritated when the people around us can't keep up. We find ourselves alienating lovers and being talked about by friends.

"I started getting really short with my friends, cutting them off in mid-sentence because I knew how important it was that I get my thoughts out before it was too late. I knew that I wouldn't live to see the day, but I wanted to make sure I did as much as I could before the government got me. I needed to leave behind instructions for everyone so they'd know what to do without me around. I'd wake up in the morning from a couple hours of restless sleep and pour out pages and pages of ideas for what life should look like after the revolution. My housemates, my girlfriend, and everyone else around in the community was getting really sick of me and telling me to chill out. I had great ideas, they said, but no one was going to listen if I was talking so fast."-scatter

We become obsessed with a million projects that are going to change or explain the world and *suddenly find ourselves fearless, convinced of our own importance, and unafraid to do things like reach out to famous people we would never have contacted if we had actually been getting enough sleep.*

"In the weeks leading up to my psychotic break I was working on an economic tract that was essentially going to re-invent Marxism for the digital age. I had actually been corresponding with John Kenneth Galbraith of all people and he had been writing back. I laugh now when I think of it. I wonder what he made of all of my sprawling pages and diagrams..." –anon.

At some point our own theories and fantasies become the worlds we inhabit, and we position ourselves in the center as messianic figures, mystics, or simply the only person who really knows...Everything we encounter fits into our own personal mythologies, which become written in the symbolic language that used to belong to our dreams but now bleeds over into our waking lives.

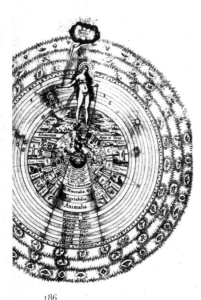

186

"I left my house at 2 am and went to the Tenderloin hunting for prostitutes, when I couldn't find any I started looking for people to talk to about my theory about the transformation of the earth into the new heaven and men and women into perfect "angel creatures." On my walk home I found a homeless man sleeping on the steps of a church and shook him awake and gave him my whole wallet with over $200 in it, because--of course, being the new Messiah, I would have no need for money, ID and credit cards any more. It all seemed so logical. The next day my wife somehow wrangled me to the hospital where (as I remember it) I underwent a sort of metaphorical crucifixion. After knocking over some equipment I was tackled by about five guys, shot up with Haldol, and strapped onto the gurney. From there I embarked on this indescribable mystical journey I like to think was probably pretty similar to what Muhammad went through. My wife doesn't quite remember it that way though... I was just mumbling and nuts."-m.l.

Sometimes our dreams become elaborate nightmares filled with conspiracies and secret languages. When we wake up months later we sometimes still find scraps of truth in the psychotic rubble.

"I ended up thinking that nanobots had been implanted into me during the surgery, and that my professors were covertly training me for my summer anthropology research abroad. I also thought I had identified a new way of communication, something animalistic and non-verbal, that was generally subconscious but noticeable through very close observation. When I describe it now, I still feel that this mode of communication exists, but I was definitely reading into people's utterances too much, deciphering subconscious admissions and clues of desire in everybody's statements. Things took on an overtly sexual set of qualities for me. I ended up in a mental ward... it was horrendous, although not as bad as before. A positive result was that I was diagnosed as manic depressive."-k

When we enter the world of hallucinations and delusions we are told we are having a psychotic break with reality and routinely hospitalized, diagnosed with a disease, and drugged. And this may save our lives. But many of us touch on similar places when we're in those frantic states, and it's hard not to wonder if the parallel perceptions we sometimes have are due to more than biochemistry. Could they actually be openings onto something real, something so powerful it tips our fragile brains over the edge? Are we getting a glimpse of systems underlying society and patterns underlying experience that most people never have a chance to see?

"I wonder how I managed not to get picked up when I wandered the streets in the sleepless nights carrying absurd items in my backpack--like every journal I've kept since I was 12, nothing practical like a jacket or a sleeping bag-- and terrified to go home because there were people living on my rooftop waiting for me to get in bed so they could jump through my skylights and kill me. Mostly, I wonder what it is that made us have such similar paranoias, the same idea that secret messages were coming through the billboards, the same notion of an impending crisis--for me it was the revolution, though I had a very different idea of what that would mean back then, and everything was so urgent because of it, the same thoughts that I was being recorded and broadcast both to audiences of random anybodies and to secret government agencies--video as well as audio, and I was sure that my fillings in my teeth and some of my jewelry were transmitting my location as well, the same conviction that there were constantly 2 or more layers of conversations going on, and that there were these other languages being used simultaneously that most people weren't even aware of.

So when I read about this stuff in your article, that you'd had very similar delusions and the like, it really got me thinking--what brought our brains, in different times, different genders, with different backgrounds and upbringings--what brought our brains into such intensely parallel thinking? Are those things somewhat universal? Are there any universals when it comes to mental health breakdowns?"-jennifer audacity

Regardless of what is revealed to us – whatever brilliance or passion is touched on in our flights through the sky—eventually our wings melt from flying too close to the sun, and we plunge into the depths of our solitary oceans of misery. At some point, due to the laws of gravity in our minds and souls, everything slips.

"My diagnosis came in June when I saw the world in crystal clear perfection on the summer solstice. I went running in the streets half naked blowing kisses to on-coming vehicles. I was locked up in a hospital and drugged pretty heavily. When I came out I still thought I understood the world more clearly than I ever had before -- living life in such an open state, moment to moment. I was then hospitalized again after visiting a friend in Philly and getting turned on to hip-hop music. After getting out of that hospital I was still feeling high for a couple of weeks, and then I crashed. My feelings of unself-consciousness gave way to deep insecurities. I moved back to my hometown.
It's been months now and I still feel bleak and hopeless. When I was manic I understood helen cixous, bjork, lacan, and talib kwel. Now I lack the concentration to read and music is dry and empty. When I was manic I hardly ate or slept. Now all I do is eat and sleep. I never used to watch TV (even before my mania). Now I find myself channel surfing. In my previous life, I loved cyborgs and donna haraway. Now I can't muster up the interest for any social theory. I don't know who I am anymore. It feels like my soul has abandoned me. I miss my passion and lust for life. I miss my curiosity. And I miss my trust in myself." -emiko

Many of us try to claw our way out with drugs and alchohol.

"I see you as someone learning to be yourself. Right now you're in a particularly ungraceful period, and that's fine. It might feel ugly, but it's fine. I've heard voices and seen things too. I've gotten exorbitantly drunk time after time after time after time. I've taken ecstasy in the middle of a depression and made myself completely suicidal after a few hours of fun, and hated myself for doing it. I've gone out and had 10 shots of tequila a few months after getting out of the psych ward, while taking depakote, and found myself projectile vomiting for days afterwards. And then more tequila when I was done.

And when I think about it, the excessive amount of crap I put in my body, from sugar to Ecstasy, really was this way to get the hell away from myself. To magically develop social skills in a crowd, or bulldoze my head out of depression for a night, or blind myself with euphoria to all the hypocrisy that seemed to be eating up my brain. To feel satsified with the people who didn't actually satisfy me, or to force a night of wild exhilaration when I felt stuck or raw and anxious, or to numb myself against the school that made me alternately want to be a superhero or a total dropout.

It just seemed like the most effective (though totally temporary) way to smother all the pain and how hard it was to live in my skin and not try to jump out, though I wouldn't have said that then. It still makes me sad to think about everything I did. There's some serious shame there." -j

For some of us the transition to depression comes as a cataclysmic crash into total hopelessness and loss of energy after weeks or months of being on fire, our minds suddenly burned out and refusing to make the simplest connections between the activities of our daily lives, rendering basic functioning next to impossible and tremendously exhausting. Some of us spend most of our time lingering for months or years in habitual states of depression that are only occasionally punctuated by mild manias. For many others the slide into depression is marked by the agitated purgatory of unbearable restlessness and confusion called a mixed state. These states, marked by both mania and depression, can be transitional or they can occur independently throughout the course of someone's life and wreak havoc.

"Here's my DSM identity - I'm an "ultra-rapid cycling" bipolar I with psychotic features and MIXED STATES! This particular manifestation of hell is profound! Mixed states are like being "tired-wired". I get jacked up with a mind that feels like it's on fire – can't stop thinking, can't stop working, can't sleep, can't eat, can't concentrate - basic mania. But here's the catch - all this occurs through the prism of extreme negativity, despondency and rage. In other words, I get manic and deeply depressed all at the same time. It is not a happy, euphoric and mind-expanding mania. It is not a sluggish and low-energy depression. It's freaking Armageddon.

Mixed states really trigger those nasty, frenzied, psychotic episodes - that incomprehensible rant at the checker in Safeway who didn't pack your grocery bag "just right," the gasoline-fueled game of speeding through a 25mph school zone at 90 mph and everybody "better get outta my way" attitude, that aggressive, fight-picking, arrest-inducing confrontation with the cop drinking his latte at Starbucks. Mixed states - amped up, enraged, deeply anti-social, and very, very dark. PS - Some people get "86"d or banned from bars and taverns. In my whacked out, suburban, pseudo-soccer mom life, I've been banned from my neighborhood grocery store, the drycleaner and post office (is that legal?). And I "look" so "normal."-anon

Often these mixed states mark the disorienting, desperate passage from the upper world to the under world. We may start witnessing the hideous shattering of all the intricate dreams we constructed when we were flying—while knowing we are utterly powerless to do anything to save them. We want so badly to keep up the pace we were managing before, but our thoughts are fragmenting and it's becoming harder and harder to explain anything to anyone. Nasty thoughts descend like frantic certainties: you can't possibly follow through on what you started, you are a failure, you are letting everyone down, you are crazy, you are doing it again. Mixed states can become very dangerous. We may lack the focus to cook ourselves dinner, but we have enough energy to jump off a bridge.

"I have all this anxious awful electricity and I can't sit still. I constantly feel like I should be doing something, but it's totally impossible to focus and I start feeling like a failed superhero. I walk around and see the sky full of birds and wonder why they all look like some kind of detached dreamworld, not real, not feeling beautiful at all, feeling like some joke of a real experience I can't have. I might feel unbelievably happy in a wired, red-eyed way for two hours and then totally apocalyptic and strung out like coming down after eating 5 pints of ice cream and all I want is to crawl out of my skin. There are occasional moments of total lucidity and astounding connections between ideas, and I cling to them like someone drowning, but then there are also moments of being curled up as small as I can get on my bed, refusing to speak or eat and determined that I should just die. I feel like my chest is going to burst with all this self-directed anger and I get violent if someone tries to touch me because I'm not worth it and I might explode—even though I would love to be touched. I just want to run away and break things. It seems more and more impossible to talk to anyone because my own hysterical accelerating soundtrack is just too overwhelming. It starts to seem more and more reasonable that I would cause everyone so much less trouble if I just died." –j

In some ways the depressions that come feel like death. The world outside us is no different than it was a few days, weeks, or months ago, but we are suddenly totally unable to participate in it.

"There is a real life, and there is living death. disinterest and disgust and nothingness. I feel it in my chest. It breaks my heart. it feels like breathlessness. being pulled from the shore... again and again and again. and every time I hear of someone else going through this, it breaks my heart even more. upon finding meaning and joy it becomes obsolete within moments. I am so sick of interacting with other human beings. as soon as I enter a conversation, I am frantically searching for a way out. since everything I believe in revolves around the importance of communication and mutual aid it leaves me as a rather high-contrast hypocrite. this assists in furthering my sense of total personal worthlessness. I am considering going back on medication. no one can live like this. what's worse is that this post will look so silly in a day or a week or whatever. I'll be like 'oh I'm fine, how stupid of me..... how uninspiring! why does it say 'go to social services' on my hand?' "-atrophy

When we are depressed the world becomes small and we find ourselves constantly disgusted with the fact that simply brushing our teeth or doing the laundry feels like such a huge task that thinking about something outside ourselves—like world politics or our next-door neighbor—seems next to impossible.

"Depression feels like shrinkage of thought and perspective. There's no comfort of Big Picture. #1 dilemma becomes how to acquire food without leaving bed, instead of how to write Great American Novel. Meanwhile, the negative thought loop gets shorter and shorter, until all it contains is something along the lines of "everything is bad, everything is bad...". You can't even be creative about why the world is a terrible place anymore. There's only the "terrible," with no meaning whatsoever. Where there's no meaning, there's no light to make out anything beautiful, and nothing will ever change. Because the world outside is a reflection of the world inside, everything drives the badness home. It often feels like being trapped inside a cylindrical 360 degree movie screen, onto which the world is projected. You become completely isolated and hideously bored. Life is like watching the same bad movie over and over. Not much action in that story. But there's one thing that always gives me a little smile of irony and the absurd afterward: the personal records that I break when I'm depressed, such as consecutive hours in bathtub, consecutive pb&j meals, number of days in same clothes, etc..." -Tiger

creating a new monotony to break free of / blue jay way / contradicting myself etc.
by Jonah Ellis

My history is one of vacant time battling occupied time. It's so hard to fill that vacancy. It's so hard to come out of a long depression, because it compels you to admit that a certain unrecoverable period of your life passed with your heart in the toilet. If you remain in that condition, you don't really have to admit that anything's wrong.

...But with all these ideals and hope for a better world, and consequently, a better life (or vice versa, depending on your chronological preference), I look forward to sleeping more than being awake pretty often. It's embarrassing. I, like so many isolated people, exist in and out of denial that there are worthy things in life that might require substantial risks. That just knowing you're right doesn't remove hurt from your life. The fact that you've raised so many new questions and challenged virtually every assumption you've ever held only makes life more difficult. This is why we long for community and friendship. To support each other as much as we mutiny against the culture that crushes us.

I guess I'm not trying to push my ideas or prove anything to anyone, though it might be a good idea. I'm just desperately trying to hold onto love as firmly as my nervous hands can. Despite the odds. Every stencil on a wall. Every plate of fries and cup of coffee beneath a long conversation at the diner. Every show flyer. Every slashed tire and broken window like writing scratched into the moon, tides creeping ever closer to the red carpet.

***This is like writing drunk, and the next day, week, month, year, whenever you emerge from it, you barely remember writing it. But you're drunk on misery, regret, hopelessness. Squished by the awfulness of it into dreams of being a small creature in an immense space, maybe an immense time. Why do I feel most alive when I'm dead? It's not what I'm feeling that seems to count, it's how much. So now I challenge whatever power, event, or misfiring

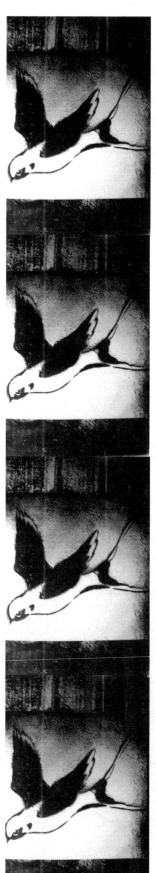

synapses (at least when I was religious, I could blame god) that cause this horror to allow me to experience hope and joy at the same level as the shit I'm in now for just one minute without having to pay dearly for it for months and years with this stubborn leech of emptiness. Fuck you, whatever you are. I will learn your tricks. I'll make it out of this mind. This mess. I'll break out with a wooden shoe-polished gun. Like John Dillinger. A dramatic escape from my attic prison. A glorious return to the people and life that I love.

I open my eyes wide and stare at the ceiling in this half-empty room, before I fall asleep, arms wanting the softness of skin and sheer curtains blowing in the breeze from a bedroom window in Savannah. The panic resurfaces from the waves. Like there was a missed opportunity at the last exit. And I've committed to the next stretch of whatever lonely highway I've accidentally ended up on. I've got the emotional stability of a high school kid watching their crush make out with someone else to "Last Night I Dreamt That Somebody Loved Me" covered by a tenth grade band in the cafeteria on talent night. How can I be this weak? War is hell. Hell is other people. Hell is trying to connect with other people and failing almost every attempt. I am at peace and at war with everything all at the same time. I am at war with this page. I'm fighting for this paragraph with military style brutality. I want it to make you love me.***

My greatest accomplishments are passing thoughts or feelings that break me out of my socially inevitable rank of "unsuccessful." Today I woke up, went to work, forgot everything that happened there by the time I arrived back at home, watched a movie, ate some leftovers, put on a record I haven't listened to in a long time and was reminded of how wonderful my friends are. This enormous feeling emerges, a simple appreciation of being alive in the present that echoes in that song between the spackled walls and plywood floor.

Depression is all-consuming and totally overwhelming.

"My depressions, when they are pure depressions, have sometimes felt like each day was going to be my last, for months on end, worrying late at night in bed that "it's all over" and that I have blown it, blown my whole life, time has caught up with me and passed me by and I've been a loser the whole way through...then waking up in the morning in the agony of the realization that yet another day has still arrived. And what am I going to do about it, what am I going to do about ANYTHING, there are ten or twenty obstacles to everything I can think to do. My morbid stacks of books and papers and the dust bunnies all over everything. My addiction to the computer and expectation that there will be anything but junk in my box if I do the addictive thing and log into my e-mail....Depression that there is no food in the house that I want to eat, but that I will not have the energy or the money to go out of the house to get something I DO want to eat. Depression that what I really might want to eat is not only expensive, but fattening. Fear of looking at my own artwork and realizing it's shit. The spines of my books reveal narrowness and immaturity instead of scholarliness. ...My clothes no longer represent who I am, or maybe I don't fit in some, or maybe I am looking at a huge dry cleaning bill. The fact that I wear socks out in three wearings and can't afford to be buying socks all the time. Not brushing my teeth.

In the past, before medication, I used to get really morbidly depressed. I would see myself as a reflection of a great historical process in which I played a rather humble and humiliated role. I would see generations of hatred between populations staring right through me. Everyone's closed off and no one questioning anything. Depression in the shape of a brand new family vehicle shaped like a teflon-coated suppository driving slowly past on a street that used to be bike-friendly. Depression an extraordinarily ugly piece of prominently placed architecture, sign of the triumph of the state over neighborhood interests. Lazy menu-writing in restaurants: the same mac and cheese, the same duck confit, the same salsa on everything. Depression is when my closest friends and lovers cannot help me and I break into tears all the time."
-eduardo

So often, depression doesn't seem to have a distinct cause rooted in the world outside ourselves. Though thoughts like the president is ordering the deaths of innocents *or* television is brainwashing the next generation *might be true—and though, when we're depressed, these thoughts might loom hideously large in our minds every waking minute of the day and overwhelm us with the sense that the world is ending—we are not this depressed* **because** *the modern world is going to hell, or because a relationship ended, or a person died—we are depressed because we are depressed. Other people walk through the same world and manage to keep functioning. Perhaps they don't feel as much as acutely. Or perhaps somewhere along the line our particular brains broke down due to a combination of culture and chemistry that is hard to pin down. Depression is different than sadness or grief or noticing atrocities. It completely takes over your life, and if it spins out of control it can make you obsess endlessly about taking your life.*

"When the depression comes it's like having lead weights on all your limbs and thoughts and feelings and emotions. It's not just being really sad. There's a big difference. The couple times it's happened to me I've stopped being able to take care of myself. I get cuts on my hands and don't tend to them even after they get infected and nasty. I get really confused and scattered—lose all sense of direction and get lost in neighborhoods I normally know like the back of my hand. I'm shut down. I stop being able to perform basic tasks like going to work and buying groceries. I stop being able to communicate with anyone because I can't even get up the energy to formulate sentences between the black noise and broken records skipping in my brain. Everything seems pointless and irrelevant because I know I'm going to be dead soon. Just imagine for a second that all of your deepest and worst insecurities have risen to the surface and are present with you wherever you go: every conversation you have has a second dialogue going on internally telling you that everything coming out of your mouth is full of shit and that you're a liar and a hypocrite and a coward and you better kill yourself as soon as you can before everyone finds out how terminally broken you really are. And then imagine that the shame of hating yourself is so great that the thoughts of ending your life are constant, like a broken record: throwing yourself in front of moving cars, jumping out of windows, gun in the back of the head, carbon monoxide in the garage, a handful of pills...it's both exhausting and horrible. And it feels like it's never going to end. I stop being able to get out of bed. I curl up in a ball and just wish that someone would come and put me out of my misery. My whole life is one big mistake. And no matter how many times I've come out of it, each new time it never feels like it's ever going to end, it feels like I'm going to be in mental agony forever." -sascha

The arc of rising and falling moods that characterizes bipolar experience does not occur with the same frequency or amplitude for everyone who lives through it. The trajectory described in the preceding pages is usually called the more classic pattern of symptoms, but it is not the only one. For some of us the depressions last months, and reach intensely morbid depths. For others, who are called rapid-cyclers by the psychiatric world, the depression might last only a few days, or even hours, followed by a mania, followed by another depression, and so on, adding up to many cycles over the course of a year. For those of us diagnosed cyclothymic, however, our lives tend to be marked by consistent stretches of a depressive mood that is less black and not as obviously disruptive, but is more persistent, and broken only occasionally by upswings into hypomania. (For more information about the different varieties of bipolar diagnosis, take a look at p. 76, where we've reprinted part of the DSM-IV diagnostic criteria.)

Contrary to popular legend, someone diagnosed with manic depression does not live in a perpetual state of madness—all forms of bipolar include periods of time when a person is not experiencing acute symptoms—a "normal" phase, if you will, between episodes—which the medical establishment refers to as a *euthymic* period. These stretches can last months and even years, even if we're not on medication—though they say the stretches become shorter and shorter the longer we're unmedicated, and even shorter if we tend to rapid cycle. These stretches can make it difficult to believe you actually have a serious problem once the memory of the worst times fades a bit—and so many people go off medication during these periods—but for most of us the mania and the depression will spring up to bite us again.

When the degree of mania and depression that we experience isn't completely extreme, and when it's haunting us more often than not, as can be the case with Cyclothymia, it can be very hard to figure out what's going on.

"I'm now trying to come to terms with my personality: my moods and my sensitivity. For me, it's hard to really pin down my cycles because I'm so caught up in them. But I've read Kay Jamison's book and I recognize that while I do have flights of energy, creativity, and nights without sleeping, I don't have such full-blown manias. I don't have hallucinatory trips "to the rings of Saturn." Hypomania seems to be what I hit.
Depression? Well, I had one major bout of depression a year ago. It had to do with grad school collapsing around me and my feeling that I had no out, no escape from my situation. But most of the time I'm just kind of "depressive". Not flat out depressed, but dealing regularly with low self esteem and poor (or at least very inconsistent) motivation. Before, I thought the waves were the world going up and down. Only a year ago did I realize it was me. Since then, I've been watching myself--my moods and my reactions. Depression and elation are there, but the hardest thing in dealing with other people are my outbursts of anger. They always seem justified, but never to the anger's recipient...
My ex-girlfriend-and-still-good-friend has said that it's painful to watch someone with my potential struggle so much. She has been urging me to see a psychiatrist for awhile… and I am coming to terms with the notion that even though I am reacting to real situations, there is an aspect of my emotions that is problematic." –NG

When you're rapid-cycling, on the other hand, the mood changes can come so fast that it seems like you're caught in a perpetual struggle between the extremes of mania and depression that can be equally hard to identify.

"I'm an ultra rapid cycler -- or, rather, it begins with rapid cycling and then, if unchecked, accelerates exponentially into ultra-ultra rapid cycling, until my life can seem a blur of just mixed states. At the time I was diagnosed, which was at my worst, I was switching between extreme states every 15 minutes to 2 hours. The mixed states would last up to 5-10 minutes. About enough time for me to get ready to commit suicide, or at one point, try to pick up where I had been interrupted before – then, BAM, I'm manic or depressed, and either don't have the interest or don't have the energy anymore to go through with it. I think the rapid cycling may actually bring a person closer to a suicidal state faster than the 'classic' months/years cycling, if only because those oh-so-dangerous mixed states are much more frequent.

I am glad to have this forum [for rapid cyclers], because as much as all those with bipolar disorder have in common, sometimes it's hard to relate well with those who have the more "classic" bipolar. I met a woman once who had that. For about 7 months she'd have depression, gain a lot of weight, not accomplish anything. Then she'd have about 3 months of near solid, practically no sleep, mania. She'd become a skeleton and paint like crazy. Then she'd maybe have a couple months to a year of remission. And as much as I understood -- and much more than your average person who doesn't know the difference between feeling down and major depression -- we had a hard time truly understanding the specifically different hues of suffering that the different types of BPD create." –Amita

When you're cycling that fast it's hard to know who you are anymore—the idea of a "real" me seems distant and hard to grasp as your whole world seems to change hourly. For some of us who are sensitive it seems that adding and withdrawing certain psych drugs from our bodies might help trigger this cycling.

"Not soon after some of the first experiments with putting me on SSRI's i started to have what both my psychiatrist and i (after my own extensive research) recognized as mixed states and rapid cycling- a feeling of extreme well being and hyper happiness would descend only to turn minutes later into extreme hopelessness, and this would happen at a dizzying rate until i was afraid to do anything- knowing that minutes later my mood would unpredictably segue into some opposite or even worse, mixed extreme like agitated happiness, or raging depression." –permafrost

While rapid-cycling can be particularly difficult to treat, no form of bipolar responds unanimously to a simple formula, no matter what the textbooks might declare. Our bodies have different sensitivities and different rhythms. Learning to take care of ourselves usually involves changing more than the combination of pills that we swallow.

"my response to all the cycling, when i was living in the city, had basically been to alternately take on tons of jobs and then when i started crashing to cancel everything and hide--so i had no accountability and NO routine whatsoever and it made it so much easier for the machinations of my brain to seem totally unbearable when things weren't actually that tragic... you know what i honestly think helped me? three things. a) got on a reasonable dose of lithium b) started working with an energy healer/body worker c) moved to a vegetable farm and started doing physical labor 10 hours a day. i was still having cycles for the first 3 or 4 months i was there, but they were much less dramatic, something more like 3 weeks semi-up and 1 week down, probably also related to monthly hormones. but I really think that having to get my ass out into the sunshine and the mud every day and work until i was tired was SO good for me, and so good for getting off that awful cycling track." -icarus

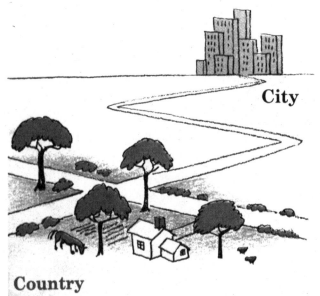

City

Country

We all have to find our own formulas, worked out over months and years of experimenting, getting to know ourselves, and listening to the demands of our restless hearts that do not want to be ignored.

When we feel we are getting closer, we must not forget that the nature of this illness is change.

Holding Lightly, Forgiving Madness by Jacks

go   gone

The sun goes down.

The sun is going down.   **The sun is** gone.

Driving home from a near run-away, I am trying to remember how to be calm. I put in a tape of a very kind Buddhist priest named Ed. He made a lot of sense a few months ago when my mind was quieter. One thought catches me: "so often we think, *if you behave well, then I will love you*. This is not fair. We cannot love this way." I nod, realize I treat myself like this all the time. My love for myself is so much more conditional than my love for anyone else. So many ifs--if you don't make any mistakes, if you don't need help, if you behave well, then I could love you. But if you don't figure it out--if you make trouble again-- so much anger. Adding something like a diagnosis of mental illness into this equation is such a tricky thing. The line between feeling that your thoughts and behavior should be something you can control and accepting or blaming it all on biology is so unclear. After I spent the eve of the millennium in a psych ward playing ping pong with a guy named Scott I swore to myself I would find out what I had to do to keep from ever ending up there again. I was so damn afraid. Nothing scared me more than becoming so devastated and out of control that I either had to kill myself or get locked up again until somebody reconfigured my brain.

About a month and a half ago the same Buddhist Ed explained that most people try, unsuccessfully, to pin down happiness by avoiding unpleasant experiences. I nodded and grinned; I was in the middle of a major upswing towards mania; I was definitely not one of them. I remember having the profound epiphany two days later that I'd arrived at such a place of blissful wisdom that not only did I require no more than a couple rocks or a scrap of paper to entertain me until the end of time, but I had also found the loophole that would allow me to slip out of my bipolar diagnosis. Clearly, I was going to flourish in a state of perpetual happiness without lapsing into the ugly black holes and the depression that broke me last time around. I didn't even need to avoid unpleasant experiences because I was so enlightened that they simply weren't going to happen. I was convinced I was going to be happy for the rest of my life.

5 days ago I found myself standing on the railing of the Golden Gate bridge deciding not to jump because a dolphin broke the surface of the ocean down below. It seemed like a sign; I should stick around on this side of mortality and re-learn how to play. I'd become so angry with myself in the last week. After a couple months evangelizing the *truth*--we can all learn to manage our brains through what we eat and how much we sleep; we don't need medication or the Man; we can control all variables and all discomfort if we have enough discipline--to anyone who would listen, I found my brain churning out black noise so fast I would ride my bike 20 miles or drive hours until I was shaking just to run away from it. I was starting to think I might make everyone's life easier if I jumped off a bridge; a few weeks before I'd felt incredibly close to God and blessed with a knowledge of how to live that was eventually going to transform everyone who met me. How could I start having these black thoughts that felt like violent insertions, like someone slipping crazy drugs in my tea, when I was still eating my oatmeal and enacting all the "lifestyle choices" that were supposed to keep me from going over the edge? Why the restless anxiety that I was about to let everyone down? When did the sight of a thousand pink clouds start

feeling like a world at the end of drugs where you're desperately trying to keep something from slipping away? The sudden certainty of loss and the urgent need to stave it off, to hold something raw and shimmery like a soap bubble in the tips of my fingers. But the connections between thoughts start snapping and so much tenuous magic turns invisible like water evaporating off hot pavement. And then all the premonitions, the forecasting dreams, the nervous hunch of impending insanity and the broken records in the brain. Sudden desire for violence, to smash and break and tear and hide and run and seize and snatch--

In the course of two weeks there was no way to sit still--as soon as darkness drops, the need to smother this raging weeping tantruming creature in my brain. I have never wanted to kill myself--I have only wanted to kill the restless blackness that comes for hours or days after the upswings and transforms my whole world and everything in it, making it nearly impossible to appreciate anything like a plant or a bird or a smile except as some sign that I'm actually ok. It is when you feel that the blackness has become your whole self that it is completely unbearable.

I would like to think that these demons don't come from me, that they are some kind of other, some black invader surging out of my DNA or last night's dinner to interrupt the *real* me at work. But I am coming to realize that I am one self. The restless demons and the visionary choirs of angels *are* me, along with the person developing between this body and this routine. I am trying to forgive myself for being exactly what I am; occasionally brilliant, frequently imperfect, mostly kind, and burdened/blessed with something in my blood that can send me divine inspiration in September along with suicidal plans in November.

When I felt myself going up this fall, despite all the changes I'd made in my diet and everything I'd tried to fix, I was still determined that I could handle myself without caving in to the Man and his medicine. I distinctly remember the day I realized I hadn't slept normally in over two months, a huge red flag. Despite all the reading I've done on bipolar disorder I still told myself, "well, I guess I just don't get to sleep like that anymore. I'll be fine. I have so much energy now anyways. I have so much to do. I'm becoming a Great Artist. I'm changing the world." I could feel the heartbeat of the city's construction hammers in my own chest; I could soliloquize on the metaphysics of a doorknob for hours. I was no longer afraid of death. Who would want to stop? But after scaring myself and my friends with the sudden need to jump off roofs or stay in bed for the rest of my life, I find myself back on medicine, opening my bills for the first time in 3 months and cleaning the neglected, rotting food off my bedroom floor.

I don't know how this will work. I don't know if I'll stay on the drugs forever or even if I'm back in safe territory. I've only been on them three days. When I woke up this morning—hours after sunrise, for the first time in ages—there was no one screaming in my head. But I still took off for the Mojave desert some hours later, possessed by a frantic need to escape, and found myself shriek-singing uncontrollably and shaking deep in my skin, flying down the highway determined to make it to Arizona by dawn--but the drugs cut my energy around 4:00 and I wound up back in my apartment, shame-faced, with my roommates shaking their heads. But I wrote this damn story in a narrow hour of sanity, fickle though it may prove to be--which seemed an impossible task even two days ago. So who the hell knows. I guess my point, to quote my roommate, is that I have to learn to be compassionate with myself, even if that means accepting that I need to medicate my brain in order to stick around on this planet. Some people tell me that diabetics just have to take insulin, and I am no different. Other people tell me psych drugs are a way of copping out on the intensity of life and becoming normalized by the screwy system. I am trying to take a more moderate piece of advice to heart--that I must hold lightly. A friend used those words in reference to a romance, but said she thought they also applied to me in my struggles to carve out a sustainable, honest life. She says we must hold lightly to our strategies, that we can't refuse to adjust our model of what works, no matter how much we'd like to reach the end of our struggles and locate *the* way out.

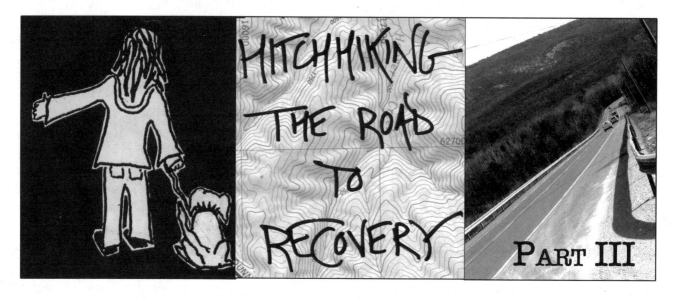

HITCHHIKING THE ROAD TO RECOVERY

PART III

Healing is a lot more than just taking drugs.
It's a wide open road

And it can be a scary one full of big ugly cars whose passengers either sneer at you or look terrified as they blow dust in your face. It's unfamiliar territory, the straight lines and narrow shoulders, the foreboding weather, the flashing billboards full of corporate drug advertisements and fast food. Are you sure you want to be on this road? Isn't there an easier way, a way where they just pick you up in a big white van and take you to a nice clean building where everyone's on the same schedule and you never have to make any decisions because the answers have already been standardized?

Maybe you should just get back to familiar territory.

But something has to change if you're ever going to face yourself and find a way to live in this crazy world. You're on a mission to learn how to take care of yourself and figure out where you belong. You're on a mission to find others who can travel with you. And things aren't always what they seem. Be patient. Remember that important rule of hitchhiking: the folks who pick you up are the ones who've been through it themselves. And we're always out there. We're keeping an eye out for you in our old beater cars and biodiesel tour vans, looking forward to some company

~

So many of the people we meet who've been labeled with mental illness or who call themselves crazy are the ones who are always looking for more or don't fit anywhere: the ones who feel rootless, displaced, unheard; the ones who wander and search and chafe; the ones who get stuck and paralyzed with nightmares and panic; the ones who drop out of college and try to make music, or ride freight trains, or lay in bed watching clouds; the ones haunted by chronic pain and mysterious maladies; the ones who hear messages no one else hears or see connections no one else can believe; the ones who are full of restlessness and desire, conviction and doubt; the ones who can't overlook the emptiness of modern life or find niches for themselves within it…

There is nothing that gnaws like loneliness. Finding community and contributing to it is a huge part of real, sustainable mental health. Emotional distress and extreme states aren't just our personal problems. They're embedded in family networks and systems of oppression, they are reproduced in our workplaces and our homes. We need to find solutions together. We need each other to become whole.

"A liberatory care practice is one in which we move beyond self-care into caring for each other. You shouldn't have to do this alone." —Yashna Maya Padamsee

Isolation almost always accompanies breakdown. One of the most important things we can do in hard times is reach out and show up, even though that often feels like the most difficult thing to do. Sometimes when you're near losing it, or when you're putting your life back together, you have to start small: attend a class once a week, make one phone call, read a book in the library instead of your bed. Sometimes you need a lot of support, and your friends can set up a care calendar where folks take turns signing up for shifts to help with the basics: cooking meals, doing housework, going for walks. Sometimes we find what we need in organized forms of peer support – Icarus groups, 12 step meetings, gatherings of the Hearing Voices network, meditation groups, and more.

> For more information on existing Icarus Project groups, check out the radical mental health contacts listed on our website. For more information on how to start your own local group, flip to the inside back cover of this book.

Our detours into "crazy" are so often full of clues and real questions. As your head clears it can be important to start paying attention to the meaning in what you've been through. The stories we tell ourselves shape so much of our experience, and how we end up feeling about ourselves. Diagnosis is just one way of putting the puzzle pieces together. Many other lenses are possible. Often it can be helpful to read books, blogs, or zines by other folks who've struggled like us to see how they're making sense of it all. When words aren't so accessible – especially when we're dealing with profound depression - we can explore our stories through other forms of expression – art, music, dance. Some of us need to communicate with our versions of gods or guides. Sometimes we need to say the questions out loud, and be heard. So often breakdowns include a lot of information about what needs to change in our lives: it might be our self-care, it might be the family systems in which we're embedded, or it might be leaving a bad job and spending more time by the sea. Though the medical establishment often encourages us to see our distress as biological and personal, so often it contains elements that are deeply spiritual and existential – what does life mean? What are we doing here? What do we do with collective trauma, with deep reservoirs of intergenerational oppression and grief? How can we be more connected to movements for justice and change? Are we trying to adjust to a sick world, or are we on a life journey of transformation? What can we change and what must we accept? How can we feel more connected to forces bigger than ourselves? How do we fill our lives with purpose and beauty? What do we do with all the information flooding into our psyches, or hiding behind walls of memory and fear.

There are so many of us out here who feel the world with thin skin and heavy hearts, who get called crazy because we're too full of fire and pain, who know that other worlds exist and aren't comfortable in this version of reality. We've been asking the difficult questions for a long time. We've been busting up out of sidewalks and blooming all kind of misfit flowers for as long as people have been walking on this Earth. Sometimes we have access to secret layers of consciousness — you could think of us like dandelion roots that gather minerals from hidden layers of the soil that other plants don't reach. If we're lucky we share them with everyone on the surface – because we feel things stronger than the other people around us, a lot of us have visions about how things could be different, why they need to be different, and it's painful to keep them silent. Sometimes we get called sick and sometimes we get called sacred, but no matter how they name us we are a vital part of making this planet whole.

Because we struggle with the extremes of madness, we often have intense empathy and sensitivity towards others: the gift of a big heart and a lot to give. Living through the "old-before-your-time survivor" and/or the "damaged dysfunctional psych patient" can also mean you become the Wounded Healer: a person who's made it through the fire and come out the other side with stories to tell and skills to share. If we can get past our fears and anxieties, it is us, not the psychiatrists and professionals, who have the knowledge and ability to connect and communicate with each other through pain into unimagined futures.

When we gather together with people who've been through what we've been through, people who share some of the mysteries and suffering that get labeled 'mental illness,' we discover new maps through crisis, learn new tools to stay healthy, and weave communities of solidarity to change the world. We discover something at the heart of our dangerous gifts: caring for others is often the best way to care for ourselves.

How can we build support networks strong enough to hold us when we go into crisis?

So often when it all comes crashing down, we find ourselves alone, and don't know what to do.

When you or someone close to you goes into crisis it can be the scariest thing to ever happen. It seems like someone's life might be at stake or they might get locked up, and everyone around is getting more stressed and panicked. Everyone knows a friend who has been there, or has been there themselves. Someone's personality starts to make strange changes, they're not sleeping or sleeping all day, they lose touch with the people around them, they disappear into their room for days, they have wild energy and outlandish plans, they start to dwell on suicide and hopelessness, they stop eating or taking care of themselves, they start taking risks and being reckless. They become a different person. They're in crisis. What the hell do you do and how do you start healing? Here's one story of impossible questions and tentative answers from Gumby, a mother trying to help her son ward off the crash and start putting the pieces back together afterwards:

" This has been the year of watching my son (16) soar and sink. Somehow, I always suspected that his brilliance didn't come without a price.

Last summer, he went 'bye-bye' for a couple of weeks. I was living in Eugene at the time, he in Portland with Dad. I knew something was up when he started calling to tell me things like, "Mom! I just realized I have only been using one eye my whole life... now I'm using both and the world looks so different!", and, "In school today I could smell every individual in my class... they each had a different scent and I could identify them all without looking at them," and *RED FLAG* "I don't need any sleep at all! I just wrote ten songs in four hours, and recorded them, all the tracks myself." Then came the crash. By the time I got to Portland, he was nearly catatonic and had forgotten how to eat, drink, or go to the bathroom. He was also having lots of conversations with Jimi Hendrix, or grieving inconsolably about women being raped and the earth being destroyed. My cousin (forced hospitalization survivor thru most of her teen years) and I stayed with him, refused the suggestions of "take him to the hospital", and basically talked him out of it for four days. He had 'lucid' moments, and they got longer and closer together, especially with a guitar in his hands. We took him to his acupuncturist/mentor, and that's when he finally cleared. We didn't know...was it a bad acid trip? Or something else? So I packed up, moved to Portland, waited...and watched.

Early this summer, a close friend of his committed suicide with methadone. My son withdrew and started to get increasingly irritated and then all-out angry with me and his dad. His dad and I have been in therapy, learning how to co-parent after ten years of divorce. We started taking our son to the therapist, feeling like he needed help dealing with his friend's death. But somewhere inside myself, I saw a train-wreck coming. He had stopped sleeping again, and I just knew. I even scheduled a psych evaluation. There was also something about his music. He had stopped playing the guitar, and was instead up all hours writing 'raps' that seemed to me incoherent nonsense rhyming (compared to his usually brilliant, cynical lyrics). He didn't make it to the appointment. A week before he was scheduled to go, I got a call from the University of Portland police. They had picked up my son on campus 'acting strangely' and had taken him to the emergency room where he was on Mental Health Watch. They CT-scanned him, drug-tested him and watched him for four hours. I then took him home. (Thankfully they didn't refuse to let me.) At five the next morning, he woke me up insisting that my house was a meth lab and that he wanted to go to his Dad's. He shoved me out of the way and ran. Next morning he got violent with his dad, punched and slapped him and threatened to leave. At that point I did a desperate thing that could have gone very badly, but ended up not... I called the police and asked them to help us get him safely to the hospital. (Believe me, it's hard to admit, as an anarchist, that I would ever call cops. Mom Panic does strange things to your ideals at times. Forgive me? I have to forgive myself... and considering the outcome, I almost have.)

So here we are, dealing with the Mental Health System, a place I was trying so hard to avoid. And yet, somehow I believed that if we could put a label on what was going on, that we could then figure out how to deal with it. He was in for two and a half weeks, on Ativan, Zyprexa, and then Depakote. And here is my treesitting-at-age-11 son asking, "How can you put me on drugs? Who am I? Crazy Duncan? or Not Crazy Duncan on Drugs?" He is struggling trying to concentrate at school, uninspired musically, and understandably mad as hell at his turncoat parents. We have to keep asking my famously impatient son to "be patient, they'll get the dosage right. You don't have to be a zombie. We promise." But can we promise that? Is it going to be either/or? Brilliant and creative or doped? I have to believe there is a balance to be struck. Oops - Gotta go...to a psych appt. Again."

The word "crisis" comes from a root meaning "judgment." A crisis is a moment of great tension and meeting the unknown. It's a turning point when things can't go on the way they have, and the situation isn't going to hold. Could crisis be an opportunity for breakthrough, not just breakdown? Can we learn about ourselves and each other as a community through crisis? Can we see crisis as an opportunity to judge a situation and ourselves carefully, not just react with panic and confusion or turn things over to the authorities?

Crisis Response Suggestions

1. **Working in Teams.** If you're trying to help someone in crisis, coordinate with other friends and family to share responsibility and stress. If you're the one going through crisis, reach out to multiple people and swallow your pride. The more good help you can get the easier the process will be and the less you will exhaust your friends.

2. **Try not to panic.** People in crisis can be made a lot worse if people start reacting with fear, control and anger. Study after study has shown that if you react to someone in crisis with caring, openness, patience, and a relaxed and unhurried attitude, it can really help settle things down. Keep breathing, take time to do things that help you stay in your body like yoga and taking walks, be sure to eat, drink water, and try to get sleep.

3. **Be real about what's going on.** When people act weird or lose their minds it is easy to overreact. It's also easy to underreact. If someone is actually seriously attempting suicide or doing something extremely dangerous like lying down on a busy freeway, getting the police involved might save their life. But if someone picks up a knife and is walking around the kitchen talking about UFO's, don't assume the worst and call the cops. Likewise if someone is cutting themselves, it's usually a way of coping and doesn't always mean they're suicidal (unless they are cutting severely). Sometimes people who are talking about the ideas of death and suicide are in a very dangerous place, but sometimes they may just need to talk about dark, painful feelings that are buried. Use your judgment and ask others for advice. Sometimes you just need to wait out crisis. Sometimes you need to intervene strongly and swiftly if the situation is truly dangerous and someone's life is really falling apart.

4. **Listen to the person without judgment.** What do they need? What are their feelings? What's going on? What can help? Sometimes we are so scared of someone else's suffering that we forget to ask them how to help. Beware of arguing with someone in crisis, their point of view might be off, but their feelings are real and need to be listened to. (Once they're out of crisis they'll be able to hear you better). If you are in crisis, **tell people what you're feeling and what you need.** It is so hard to help people who aren't communicating.

5. **Lack of sleep is a major cause of crisis.** Many people come right out of crisis if they get some sleep, and any hospital will first get you to sleep if you are sleep deprived. If the person hasn't tried Benadryl, herbal or homeopathic remedies from a health food store, hot baths, rich food, exercise, or acupuncture these can be extremely helpful. If someone is really manic and hasn't been sleeping for months, though, none of these may work and you may have to seek out psychiatric drugs to break the cycle.

6. **Drugs are also a big cause of crisis.** Does someone who takes psych meds regularly suddenly stop? Withdrawal can cause a crisis. Get the person back on their meds (if they want to transition off meds they should do it carefully and slowly, not suddenly) and make sure they are in a safe space. Meds can start working very quickly for some, but for others it can take weeks.

7. **Create a sanctuary and meet basic needs.** Try to de-dramatize and de-stress the situation as much as possible. Crashing in a different home for a few days can give a person some breathing space and perspective. Perhaps caring friends could come by in shifts to spend time with the person, make good food, play nice music, drag them outside for exercise, spend time listening. Often people feel alone and uncared for in crisis, and if you make an effort to offer them a sanctuary it can mean a lot. Make sure basic needs are met: food, water, sleep, shelter, exercise, if appropriate professional (alternative or psychiatric) attention.

8. **Calling the police or hospital shouldn't be the automatic response.** Police and hospitals are not saviors. They can even make things worse. When you're out of other options, though, you shouldn't rule them out. Faced with a decision like this, get input from people who have a good head on their shoulders and know about the person. Have other options been tried? Did the hospital help in the past? Are people overreacting? Don't assume that it's always the right thing to do just because it puts everything in the hands of the "authorities." Be realistic, however, when your community has exhausted its capacity to help and there is a risk of real danger. The alternative support networks we need do not exist everywhere that people are in crisis. The most important thing is to keep people alive.

Advance Directives

If you know your crises get bad enough to get you into a hospital, there is a tool you should use called an **Advance Directive**. Basically it's like a Living Will for crisis, it gives you power and self-control over what happens to you when you go into a crisis. If you start to lose your mind and have a hard time speaking for yourself, people will look at your Advance Directive to figure out what to do.

There is an elaborate Advance Directive form at the Bazelon legal center you can use at http://www.bazelon.org/issues/advancedirectives/templates.htm, or you can just write a letter and sign it. Write down who you want contacted if you are in crisis and who you don't want contacted, what hospital you prefer to go to, what medications you do and don't want to be given, what health practitioner you want to work with, and any special instructions, such as "take me out into the woods" or "help me sleep with these herbs or those pills," "feed me kale," or "when you ask me questions, give me a long time to answer, be patient and don't walk away" or "make sure I can see my pets as soon as possible."

Write your directive up, get it signed by someone and write 'witness' by their name, and date it. Put copies somewhere that your closest people know where it is and where to get it (with a therapist or health practitioner, with family, with people close to you, people in any support or activist group you're in). Then when you go into crisis, people can use your directive as a guide on how to respond to the situation, and it can be used to help convince hospitals, doctors, etc to respect your choices on how to be treated. (Directives have some legal weight, but not as much as a living will. Ongoing reforms in mental health law may strengthen the role of directives in the future.)

On Suicide

While it's easy to romanticize certain sides of bipolar disorder, it is a dangerously incomplete picture: if you believe the statistics, 1 in 5 untreated manic-depressives commit suicide. In the medical establishment's opinion, bipolar disorder is a highly lethal disease. Whether or not you choose to see things this way, the stark fact remains that the extremes of bipolar mood swings have driven thousands and thousands of people to kill themselves, and these swings can happen with astounding speed.

There is no accepted theory about why one person who is suicidal ends up doing it and another doesn't. There is no perfect answer to what you should do when someone is suicidal, and no reliable way to prevent someone from killing themselves if they really want to. Suicide is, and will probably always be, a mystery. There are, however, a lot of things that people have learned, things that come from a real sense of caring and love for people who have died or who might die, and truths people have realized when they were at the brink and made their way back. Here are a few we've collected:

1. Feeling suicidal is not giving up on life. Feeling suicidal is being desperate for things to be different. People are holding out for a better person they know they can be and a better life they know they deserve, but they feel totally blocked. Discover what the vision for a better life is, and see how it is only possible to realize it if you stick around to find out what can happen. Turn some of that suicidal energy towards risking change in life. Find out what behavior pattern or life condition you want to kill instead of taking your whole life. Is there a way to change those patterns that you haven't yet tried? Who can you turn to for help changing those patterns?

2. People who are suicidal are often really isolated. They need someone to talk with confidentially on a deep level, someone who is not going to judge them or reject them. Did something happen? What do you need? Be patient with long silences, let the person speak. Let people ask for anything, an errand, food, a place to stay, etc. Often suicidal people really don't want to be honest because they're so ashamed of what they are feeling and it is an incredibly hard thing to admit. Be patient and calm.

3. People need to hear things that might seem obvious, like: You are a good person. Your friendship has helped me. You are a cool person and you have done cool things, even if you can't remember them now. You have loved life and you can love it again. There are ways to make your feelings change and your head start working better. If you kill yourself, nothing in your life will ever change. You will hurt people you love. You will never know what could have happened. Your problems are very real, but there are other ways to deal with them.

4. Suicidal people are often under the sway of a critical voice or belief that lies about who and what they are. It might be the voice of a parent, an abuser, someone who betrayed you, or simply the twisted bleak version of yourself that depression and madness have put in your brain. Usually this voice is not perceiving reality accurately -- **get a reality check from someone close** and stop believing these voices. You aren't a "failure," and change isn't impossible. And **You Are Not Alone** -- Other people have felt pain this deep and terrible, and they have found ways to change their lives and survive. You are not the only one.

5. **There are ways to get past this and change your life.**

"Sometimes wanting to kill yourself just means you don't want to live the life you are living and you can change your life with that power - cuz what the hell - you were about to Lose your whole life - so why not instead Lose your school/job/pretenses/fears/adherence to society's standards/shame. I have found some of my suicidal episodes to be strangely liberating in that way. I wouldn't take back any of what made me who I am today.

Vent Endure Survive. Sometimes you can thrive and bloom like a flower but sometimes your goal is just to exist and survive like a cactus."

Strikes me sometimes like growing and learning is all about sowing the meaning back into everything you care about after it's been sucked out and spit on the ground, delving deep and finding your empowerment everywhere you look: from the painful and scary to the ludicrous and beautiful.

your existence

is appreciated

"So the drugs aren't evil. No really, I swear. It has to do with harnessing energy, holding on it, and letting it out when you want -- not letting the brilliance you have block out the s and send you over to the other side. Psychos is like catching on fire and just letting yourse burn. It leaves scars. And at some point it becomes harder and harder to put the piece back together. Having control over your powe is going to become more and more important you get older, and less and less easy to do. Tru me on that one. There are lots of different places in your brain that don't always need t talk to each other. It's okay to forget things sometimes, even for decades. Just let them res Don't try to hold on to all those amazing imag and thoughts and plans if you feel them slipping, they'll come back when you need them, when you're ready to handle them. It doesn't all have to make sense right now. I guarantee you'll understand it all more later o

42

you're not alone

HOMEMADE HOT AIR BALLOON →

TELESCOPE →

SHARK ↓

It's good to have a map, even if you know your way around. It helps to get you on those back streets, taking shortcuts that take twice as long. I used to have a red pencil, and I'd mark the streets as I walked, trying to eventually have walked on every street. Maps help give you a different sense of perspective on your town and your place in it. Makes you look at it and its possibilties in new ways. -cindy

seeds

Plant them.

They grow.

DON'T GIVE UP

There are a lot of big gaping questions on our minds these days, such as:
what can we do for our friends in times of extreme crisis to keep them from either getting locked up or hurting themselves?

Here's a dialogue from the members of The Icarus Project: www.theicarusproject.net

how to support   By: fireweed

a friend has just broken down. it's been days since she's slept, her brain won't stop, and she thinks the only way to end it is to kill herself. we've got herbalists flying off into the night to bring her their potions and someone is getting some tranquilizers so that she has a full range of options for short-term fixes. i'm about to head over and spend time with her.

we're going to support her in radically requestioning her diet (sugary, and bread) and we're committed to sticking by her.
question is: what shall we do? and how might what we do differ if she's flying or then if she plunges?
i have a basic trust that love will find a way, and a small amount of practical knowledge in intuitive healing. anyone who has more experience, being manic or midwifing the spirit of those who are, any ideas on what we can do? what have you liked? what has worked?

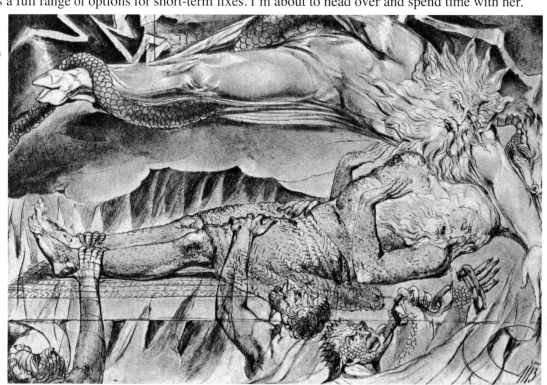

the right person for the job
By: Eduardo

what works for me, and seems to work for my bipolar girlfriend, is unflinching care and nurturing. i say that and i never use the word nurturing. it's what i crave when i'm not well and the only thing that calms me down. also an environment where everything doesn't have to be perfect and in its neat little place.
the breakdown has to be permitted. Looking down on ourselves because we can't 'keep up' with either the rest of the world, when we're low, or our own thoughts and aspirations when we're 'up,' is enough of a condemnation to misery without the baffled gaze of others making it worse. Anyone with too clear ideas of what normal is or should be can actually worsen the sufferer's self-esteem.
the only thing that seems to help me is a certain amount of pampering from the people I've selected to really care about me. This does not always or even usually include self-assigned closest relations such as the biological ones. A former heroin addict who is not bipolar can have more insight and clemency and be a better influence than a brother who occasionally takes Prozac or a parent who is a licensed psychologist. Holding people is good. Visiting them is good. Knowing that people care is about as much help as I can take when I'm off the charts up or down.

also.. by: andytoomajian

fireweed, since you mentioned herbalists and potions i wanted to throw out there the possibility of using california poppy tincture as a means to calming manic states. california poppy contains a lot of milder opiate analogues and is used as a bedtime sleep aid and also as a febrifuge (helps break fevers). now, different people have different experiences of the plant and the tincture, and some find it totally mild and gentle. however, for me, it was too much.

however, jacks (who was my housemate for the past year) tried some as a way to zonk out when she was in manic states and told me she found it pretty effective. what i remember ashley saying about it was that when her brain was spinning too fast all she really wanted was for it to stop so she could fall asleep and that the poppy tincture helped with that. maybe she'll weigh in more on her experience with this.

a few words on poppies and patience   by: Jacks

hmmm... i feel like the ol' pessimist on the site these days.   but i'll launch ahead. i did try the poppy tincture for a little while last fall when i was getting manic, and it seemed to help for a couple days, but the next week i hit a place where i could take twice as much poppy as my 250 pound roommate, pop 3 or 4 benadryls, have a shot of alcohol, and i was still up till 5 conversing with god and the plants, waking up at 6:30 and dashing off to feel the city's construction hammers echoing through my chest with all the other crazy synchronous thoughts, and 2 or 3 weeks later my head had gotten so fast i was climbing up on the golden gate bridge to see if i should jump. the thing that brought me down was zyprexa. nasty old anti-psychotic. borage and poppy and love and attention and no sugar didn't do it. i'm not saying they won't work for other people. just wasn't enough for me. i had to cave in and see a shrink.

A Note: Since this dialogue was originally published, we have learned a lot more about alternatives in handling crisis and the dangers of rushing to use psychiatric medications. We have met many people who have in fact come back from manic and psychotic states with the help of alternative remedies such as acupuncture, homeopathy, trauma-related therapies, shamanic work, retreat, self-help groups, and time and patience. At the same time, more and more studies are released every day indicating that atypical anti-psychotic medications, and zyprexa in particular, are even more dangerous than previously acknowledged, causing side-effects such as metabolic syndrome, diabetes, obesity, chronic illness, and even death, in a significant number or users. We believe that the decision to treat mental crisis with psychiatric meds, and anti-psychotics in particular, is an extremely loaded choice that should not be undertaken without careful consideration and research into the potential dangers and alternatives.

For more information, check out some of the following resources:
Madness Radio: http://madnessradio.net
The Harm Reduction Guide to Coming Off Psychiatric Drugs, co-published by The Icarus Project & the Freedom Center.
Mad in America: Bad Science, Bad Medicine and the Enduring Mistreatment of the Mentally Ill, by Robert Whitaker.
The Mad in America website.
Healing the Split: Integrating Spirit into Our Understanding of the Mentally Ill, by John Nelson.
Coming Off Psychiatric Drugs, ed. by Peter Lehmann

How do you "talk sense" into someone who refuses to believe they have any kind of problem?

It's really hard. Sometimes people have to crash and burn to figure things out. But it's important to try anyway—when we're flying through the sky we need some mile-markers back on Earth. Even if we're not ready to hear you clearly, your words stay with us. These are the words one of Sascha's friends sent him when he was convinced that the last thing he needed was help:

never

"He will never get me."

"you say that you don't need to slow down--it may be true that you're "fast for a reason right now" but the first thing that comes to my mind is a quote i heard once: "speed is the enemy of democracy." and inversely, speed is the friend of capitalism (whether it is cause or result is questionable). but it is virtually impossible to work with people when you're going too fast to communicate with them. i found it so hard to listen to people when i was crazy--so many other things were demanding my attention, sounds that others couldn't hear, and i chose for a while to focus on the sounds of the billboards and the pop songs rather than people i knew, and that was wrong. we know who makes those, and i think it's the enemy. i don't want to give the enemy more attention than people i love and who love me...." – jennifer audacity

Dealing With Shrinks/Dealing With Hospitals

So we're about to give you a whole bunch of suggestions that will help you get better informed about the places you might need to turn for help if things get really out of hand. If you feel like you're headed that way, **write down your own plan when you're in a clear head space** and give it to a friend you really trust. If your mind is moving like molasses and there's a repeating tape loop in your head saying that you don't deserve to live, it's very hard to advocate for yourself or have the patience to be put on hold for long periods of time or sit in waiting rooms for hours. Chances are that if you get so far lost you need a hospital or serious psychiatric intervention, you might not be able to handle the whole bureaucratic process yourself.

So where do you turn if you feel like you're ready for some medical intervention? If you just want to talk, you can look for a therapist. If you think you might need medication, you'll need to see a psychiatrist. Psychiatrists these days are very expensive and usually see patients for a half hour to consult on meds. Therapists usually give you an hour to talk over your problems and can't prescribe meds. The best way to find these folks is through word of mouth referrals. But when no one knows any good practitioners, you can try to find a decent mental health clinic in your area. If you can find yourself a good case worker or advocate much of this process will be a lot easier. If you find yourself getting put on long waiting lists and being tangled in frustrating webs of bureaucracy when trying to get an appointment at a clinic, a good trick is to ask to speak to the clinical director. Remember that the folks behind the desk deserve your respect, but that it's their responsibility to help you get what you need. Trying to get appointments with shrinks or therapists in private practice usually entails a long wait, depending on where you live—often as much as 6 weeks—but might be the only route to go if you're trying to get reimbursed by health insurance. If you feel like you really need help now but your brain is too much of a mess to handle the frustrating process of trying to get an appointment somewhere, swallow your fears and be really honest with a friend, family member, co-worker, whoever you can turn to, and ask them to make the phone calls for you.

"When I first knew I was breaking down I started calling up psychiatrists but the process was so impossible I had no idea what I was doing. No one had any time to see me unless I was on the edge of suicide. I would cry for an hour after every unsuccessful phone call and finally gave up completely. I started the phone calls again after a couple weeks, but by the time I actually got in to see someone my mind had deteriorated so much that I ended up in the hospital 2 days later. I wish I'd asked someone to help me but I was way too ashamed and just felt like I was weak."

If you have an inkling that something funny's going on in your brain, which you most likely do since you've got this book in your hands, do as much of your own research as you can before you go see a psychiatrist or a therapist so you'll be familiar with the words they use, the diagnoses they might suggest, and the treatments they'll recommend. It's so important when walking into a doctor's office for the first time to feel empowered as much as possible. You have to remember that they're here to help you, even if everything seems clinical and intimidating. **If at all possible, bring a friend to help advocate for you, or at least to hold your hand in the waiting room!** Once you're inside you will most likely see tons of free samples from drug companies and outlandish things like Prozac pens, as well as lots of diplomas and enormous books. It may seem terrifying or ridiculous to tell this person about your life history. Know they don't have all the answers and any diagnosis they give you can't sum up your soul. But they have access to one possible tool in your toolkit, and if you want to try meds, this is your gatekeeper.

"It's just a simple Rorschach ink-blot test, Mr. Bromwell, so just calm down and tell me what each one suggests to you."

46

Questions for Potential Psychiatrists and Therapists

How long have you been practicing?
Do you have experience treating the issues I'm dealing with?
Do you yourself have personal experience of mental illness with your self, friends, or family?
Have you ever worked on a psych unit? Do you have experience working with people in crisis?
Are you familiar with alternative therapies and are you comfortable combining them with medication?
(if this is an issue) How do you feel about my ambivalence towards taking psych drugs?
Why did you become a mental health worker?
What is it about your work you like?
Where has your work been ineffective?

Hospitals

No one wants to end up in a mental hospital, but sometimes it is the only option currently available for someone in a state of extreme crisis. In certain parts of the country, exciting small projects are opening that offer non-coercive sanctuaries for people in crisis – check out Soteria House Alaska, Soteria Vermont, and Second Story in Santa Cruz, CA for examples. We need a lot more of these! In an ideal world there would be a network of beautiful safe houses everywhere full of nurturing friends, creative activities, and organic food, but unfortunately this is something we need to work to create instead of something that is a widespread reality. For now many of us are stuck with psych wards.

What kind of "extreme crisis" justifies ending up as an inpatient somewhere? The answer really varies depending who you ask. For the mental health establishment you must be "a danger to yourself or to others." Perhaps the simplest definition is that you cannot take care of yourself at all—you're intensely suicidal, delusionally manic, or in some other combination of hell that renders you past the point of all functioning. You need a safe place where you're not going to hurt yourself and you're not going to have to be responsible for anything, and your friends and family may not be able to provide this. At some point they may be overwhelmed, or there may be no one to take care of you, and you might need some medical intervention to derail total catastrophe—in the world we live in, the hospital may become the only alternative.

One thing to keep in mind is that even if you're terrified of having to go to the hospital, if it's seeming like you might end up there at some point anyway, it's wise to **pick a hospital that you can live with** – not the one that the police bring you to in restraints. You might want to designate a friend or family member to help deal with the bureaucracy and advocate for your rights should the time come. Hospitals are miserable places to end up, but it's usually a very temporary situation and there are ways you can make the best of it and learn lessons to keep you from having to end up back there.

If you're doing the research for yourself or for a friend to find the best hospital around, here are a few things to ask: Can your friends have easy access to visit you? If you already have a doctor you trust, can your doctor consult on your care? Can any other outpatient providers (counselors and therapists) be involved in decision making? Do patients have access to the outdoors, decent food, alternative therapies, or books?

Know your rights!

If you end up in the emergency room, no hospital is allowed to refuse you treatment due to lack of funds if you're in a state of extreme crisis—they should push through Emergency Medicaid. But this also means they can commit you against your will if you decide to back out in the waiting room and they've decided you need treatment.

Not everyone who ends up in the psych ward checks themselves in voluntarily. We're encouraging you to get real about the problems in your head *before* you end up getting dragged in by an authority figure of one form or another. If it's decided that your judgment is impaired and you are too dangerous to yourself or others to walk the streets, you can be incarcerated against your will; this is called a "5150 hold." During this time you have no right to refuse drugs or

Name: Sascha Dubral

I am on Level : ●   ■

Activity Privileges:
Level 1: Title 15 Privileges only
What I need to do to get to Level 2:
Stop inappropriate, self-destructive behaviors
Wear clothes and use toilet appropriately
Be sexually appropriate
Do not act on impulse; talk to staff
Comply with rules of the unit

On Level 2 I can choose from 2 of the following:
(pending staff availability and approval)
☐ The viewing of a television program or a specific video
☐ Decaf coffee/tea socialization groups (with cookies)
☐ Additional appropriate reading materials
☐ Extra grooming activities, including the supervised use of an electric razor
☐ Exercise/aerobic groups
☐ Ping pong, basketball or other games
☐ Playing musical instruments
☐ Additional time in the outdoor recreation area/ "sun time"
☐ Extra out-of-room time in general
☐ Additional telephone calls
What I need to do to get to Outpatient:
Practice good self-care (brush teeth daily, bathe when given the opportunity)
Practice appropriate behaviors that show self-control, including talking to staff members when problems arise, replacing bad thoughts with good thoughts, using exercise as a way to release anger.
Talk with staff about symptoms that are present (voices, fears, hyperactivity) and accept appropriate treatment.

For privileges on FOP speak to your therapist

DIS/NOVER 6/99

treatment. The psych team has 24 hours to decide whether to release you or try to make you stay in the hospital; usually they'll try to convince you to sign yourself in voluntarily. If you're checked in voluntarily, you have the right to refuse drugs and the right to check yourself out. If you won't agree, and they still think you're a hazard, they can recommit you involuntarily for 72 hours—this involuntary commitment can be extended indefinitely as long as the treatment team can substantiate their reasons for doing so. The only way to overturn them is to win a hearing with a judge.

Honestly, time spent in a hospital can be excruciatingly miserable, in no small part because you had to be in a pretty bad state to end up there in the first place; it can be boring and barely remembered through a haze of psych drugs; it can feel incredibly claustrophobic and horribly depressing; it can be a welcome respite from the pressure of trying to keep together a daily appearance of normality around functioning people; it can feel like you're being held hostage by a bunch of patronizing doctors who have no idea what you're talking about; it can feel like a cinderblock prison full of zombies; it can feel like a collection of people whose versions of reality are too bizarre and interesting to be walking the streets; it can feel like hell or it can feel like the most necessary calm in the eye of a storm.

But no matter how you experience it, hospitalization is temporary; you will make it through and tell the tale. If you're determined, getting hospitalized can be the first step in making a serious commitment to healing yourself and listening hard to what your soul needs to live out all its crazy dreams. **Your spirit is not dead**. If you make it through this you will be strong as hell—and you will be able to help so many people. Don't give up.

"I had this vision in the hospital… I was still pretty manic but I was so dulled down from all the drugs that it was hard to think clearly about much of anything or remember who I was. I was beginning to despair, wondering if I'll ever have my life together again or feel passion about anything.

So here's the memory: I've just come from the med line and I lie back in bed. I've slickly pocketed the depakote and as I'm lying there with its blood level decreasing in my system, I can feel this power inside of me that I'd forgotten was there, literally feel it welling up and pouring out of me without its suppression from the drug. Then I have one of those half-dream images. There are a bunch of other people in the room, patients and hospital workers and doctors and I know they can't see it, but I close my eyes and I feel weeds growing all around my bed, vining and trellising plants, bunch grass, and dandelion flowers. I can feel the wild still in me even amidst the sterile hospital walls. It's my little secret and I grin to myself. And even though I know the road is going to be hard, I know for that moment that in the end everything is going to be alright."-Sascha

Taking Control of Our Mental Health Part III—Committing to Taking Care of Ourselves

What do you do with your life now?

Part of being diagnosed bipolar is realizing you have to make serious changes to keep from ending up in the same holes over and over again. You have to start taking care of yourself and making your health a priority, even if the people around you have less fragile systems and can sustain a more punishing lifestyle. And when you're trying to crawl out of the hardest places, your health needs to be the biggest priority in your life, even if you think you don't have time for it, even if you define yourself as someone who stays up all night and drinks coffee and smokes cigarettes instead of eating meals, even if lots of people depend on you. You must carve out some time to heal.

The diagnoses they give us are useful to a degree—they allow us to navigate the system, and if we do our research and read up on the words they're using they can allow us to make good choices about getting medical help when we need it—pharmaceutical drugs that might overpower the demons or the depression, or therapy that might help us get a clear look at our history. But drugs and doctors are only the beginning—once you know you have this delicate, powerful, and potentially devastating tendency in your blood, you need to start looking at yourself as a whole person and start seeking ways to heal your body and mind. You need to define for yourself what healthy means, what an "appropriate level of functioning" is for *you* and your beliefs, and then try to take what you can from any tradition that might help you get there, whether it's Western medicine or Chinese herbs. We're going to talk about psych drugs in the next section, but for right now we want to focus on the things **you** can do to help yourself.

Patience, Hope, and Holding On

The weeks and months after a serious crash or a period of intense cycling are fragile, slippery, and frustrating. Things will start getting better, but whether you're taking Depakote or herbal tinctures, nothing is going to fix you immediately. If you choose to go on medicine it often takes months to find a combination and dosage that works, and you will probably have a bunch of side effects at first—often they will taper off after a few weeks. For people more prone to rapid-cycling, the introduction and withdrawal of various medications can intensify cycling for a while. You might feel much better for a week and then hit a low again. You might have to change doctors or acupuncturists or schools. You might not make any sense to the people who love you and consistency might seem like a castle in the clouds. This process requires patience, persistence, and a lot of hope. But know that so many of us have been there before, riding the strange strung-out purgatory between the flights and falls of madness and the awkward days of re-learning to walk—and eventually we all remembered how to dance.

One Good Day

First you need to focus on getting through each individual day. Just that. Keep it slow and simple. It's so much easier to take care of things before they get totally out of hand then it is to do the damage control after the fact—so start with the basics. Try making a list of things you HAVE to do everyday to keep yourself healthy. These are things that are actually MORE important than all those projects you wish you were doing or all those people you want to be hanging out with—you need to do this stuff first. This was the list they gave Sascha in the halfway house last time around:

a) **get enough sleep**
b) **eat enough good food**
c) **take my drugs**
d) **go to work**
e) **exercise**
f) **talk to friends**

These are some of the really important basics that you should consider putting on your list, but you'll probably want to come up with some of your own. The important thing is that you have structure to refer back to when you mind is slowly unclouding and basic routine is something that can orient you. This way, if you're feeling off, you can go through the list and figure out if there's anything that you might have forgotten to do.

Routine

"I've been so confused, cycling (or so they tell me, I just know I spent 45 straight hours in bed with no energy but so many ideas I couldn't keep track of my head), trying to figure out how to "manage" this shit. Trying to decide if I should keep living in my wonderful crowded chaotic punk house or go somewhere a little more mellow and discipline-friendly. How important has getting on a schedule been for people? How important has discipline been? i.e. how much of my live-only-in-the-present-all-night-projects-dumpstering-extravaganza life can I hold onto?"-eris

Across the board it seems that **Having a Stable Routine is Really Important** for folks who are trying to put their lives back together. A set time to get up in the morning, a set time to go to sleep at night, and a relatively organized and consistent set of things to do during the day.

"For me, caring, supportive, challenging environments, a fairly consistent routine of eating sleeping exercising and herbing, and some responsibility or situation where my presence is necessary and desired, these are all things that, while in the depths of a severe depression won't have an outwardly visible immediate or dramatic effect that any number of meds would, but they WILL serve as the almost invisible underpinning of increased well-being that I may not even be able to see until they've been "on board" for several months."-permafrost

steps

Taking Care of The Basics

eating well

sleep & rest

ONLY $2.99!

exercise

herbs, meds, etc.

having a schedule

1: BAND PRACTICE 3: TRAPEZ LESSONS 7: EAT 8: SLEEP!

REFILL 3 weeks ago.

FISH OIL

SOPHIE CRUMB .05

One of the big distinctions it seems important to make is between the needs of someone who's in a crisis period and trying to get their life together and the needs of someone who's relatively stabilized.

"i don't exactly have a schedule now, but the biggest thing is i try to get 8 hours of sleep every night. And i save staying up past 12 for an occasional thing, not a consistent thing. And what i've always found is that the longer i'm stable the more flexible i can get with my schedule, but that when i'm coming out of hell i have to be more consistent about going to bed at a reasonable hour and showing up somewhere every day to work or get my hands dirty. You do not need to be a member of the 9 to 5 beehive to be functional."-icarus

A lot of people who are bipolar have a hard time focusing on everyday work, and that probably explains partially why so many of us naturally gravitate towards subcultures with standards of living that deviate from the mainstream. While having a lifestyle where more freedom is permitted, like being self-employed, or where very little money is needed, like living in a collective house, dumpster-diving, riding freight trains and hitchhiking etc., might feel more true to your soul and who you eventually want to be, when you're coming out of a crisis it's often much easier to get your life together if you accept a little structure from the outside, whether in the form of a consistent job or regular yoga classes.

Work can be really healthy sometimes – it builds self esteem, teaches us lessons about having to get along with other people, and directs our energy away from the problems in our brains and towards something outside ourselves. When you're in a rut it's an excuse to get out of the house.

Another note about routine—our routines aren't limited to some major activity we do for 8 hours every day. Making little routines for yourself, whether it's drinking a cup of tea every day at 5:00, checking in with your seedlings, or riding your bike to the library, can be so helpful. Make plans to check in with a friend every Tuesday, sign up for a dance class and actually go twice a week, join a group like Food Not Bombs and cook food with a group of people every Friday, play online bingo, whatever it takes to know you've got some commitments to keep and some deliberate moments to punctuate your days.

out

Out of the house
Outdoors   Outside

Exercise

It's seems pretty obvious that a huge factor in so many people feeling so crazy all the time is that our society has "evolved" to the point where most people don't have to use their bodies for work anymore. That means most of us spend a lot more time in our heads, which isn't necessarily always the best place to be!

Physical exercise can be one of the most important aspects of anyone's mental health.

"One of the most important things I ever did, when I wasn't even sure I wanted live and felt out of mind self-conscious and alienated from other people, was start draggin' my ass to an incredibly intense Capoeira Angola class. I was completely lost but fully engaged and absorbed in learning the difficult movements...for the time I was in the class I entered a truly transcendent space where all I could hear was my breathing and all the insidious poison negative thought loops completely receded- there simply wasn't room for them.

Studies show that exercise at least 3x a week is a better anti-depressant than any of the SSRI's, and the mood-elevating effects kick in quicker and last longer. And it comes from you, not a pill, which is a very different high. Even when happiness or peace still seems elusive you can gird yourself with the sense of achievement in making physical progress, not to mention zero side-effects and detoxing yourself from years of accumulated pharmaceutical build-up. Try pursuing a class with a reputable teacher of chi gong, tai-chi, yoga --or if you're up to something more energetic, a dance class you have always wanted to take. At least these are pro-active healing modalities and not passive recipient-healer set ups. It's good to have

51

a balance of both in your life- even at your sickest.

And also- don't set yourself up for failure, start with a small goal and get support for it from family, friends or therapist. Also, joining a class is much much easier when you're seriously depressed than trying to focus on something alone- every time you quit you'll beat yourself up- you're much less likely to do so when surrounded by a bunch of other people with a teacher to focus on." -permafrost

Even if sports aren't something you've ever been into, using your body can make a big difference in your life.

A few words from the kid who always got picked last on the teams and didn't climb a tree till he was 15: I always associated exercise with the jock kids in my school, and I hated them. I always felt really awkward and shameful of my body. I hung out with the punks, and we were too cool to play sports. Quitting smoking cigarettes and swimming everyday when I was 22 years old saved my life. Everything's so connected –personally, I've learned to go running when my mind is starting to race – exhaust myself, burn up some of that manic energy so that my body can't help but fall asleep when I need it. And I get so much of my best thinking done when I'm running or swimming. I discovered some years ago that YMCA's are actually really cool places that give you access to a whole diverse community of people who are all striving to be healthy. They have affordable scholarship memberships, and once you have a card you have access to any YMCA in the country. Having a place to exercise and take a shower every day has been so good for me at times when my life at home or on the road has been really chaotic.

Exercise doesn't have to be something you set aside as a separate activity – you can make it part of your daily work whether you're doing construction or digging in the dirt. You can do simple things like walk or ride a bicycle rather than drive. You can take the stairs rather than the elevator. Stretching in the morning is a simple way to reconnect with your own muscles and calm your mind. Just remember that you are a whole person and not just a brain and finding balance involves healing all of you.

Sleep

Sleep is usually one of the first things to go at the beginning of a manic cycle and one of the only things we can manage to do when we're miserably depressed. Sleep can clue us in to where we are on our personal ups and downs—you might notice that when you're starting to get manic you stay up later and later, or wake up earlier every day. You might notice that being unable to get out of bed every morning or wanting to crawl back into bed by sunset means you're starting to get depressed.

Having regular sleep cycles is definitely key to holding ourselves together. Those of us who are bipolar seem to have really sensitive "internal clocks" and losing even a single night's sleep can disrupt our whole rhythm and start us down that path to mania. Don't ban yourself from the space after midnight forever—just think of it as a powerful place to visit that isn't safe to stay. Staying up late can be intoxicating and some of the best ideas and most amazing experiences seem to come out of that edge space, but if we let ourselves go there too often or for too long we're likely to end up in trouble—walking around feeling the whole world creeping under our fingernails and unable to shut off our brains. Good sleep is important to everyone, but to us it's *precious*.

"Sleep deprivation is such a problem that before modern treatments were available, roughly 15 percent of manic patients lost their lives to physical exhaustion." (From *Bipolar Disorder Demystified*, p. 170)

How do you get yourself better sleep when you need it?
Here are a few suggestions that don't involve psych drugs: get more exercise during the day, opt out of activities that start late at night, drink herbal teas like chamomile and scullcap, tie something over your eyes to keep the light out in the morning, run a constant noise like a fan or a noise machine, ask a friend for a back-rub before bed, set regular times that you go to bed and wake up that correspond to daylight and stick to them, don't start fascinating activities after 8:00 PM.

And what about psych drugs?
All the methods we listed above might help us out when things aren't too serious, but don't necessarily do the trick for everyone when we're really having problems. For some of us, taking psych drugs for sleep seems to make sense when it's an emergency; for others, taking them at the first signs of a problem keeps us from hitting the stage where we really crash. Once you get to know yourself well, you might notice one day that you've been hearing three cds playing in your head for the last 48 hours, your eyes are getting wilder, and your words are getting faster every time you talk. For you this usually means you're starting an upswing—but if you take an extra pill to help you sleep tonight it might disrupt the process. You have to get to know yourself and recognize when things like trans-continental plane flights or nasty breakups or the first day of summer mean you're likely to get triggered and might want to start getting extra sleep sooner rather than later. And if you find that these drugs are helping you, it might be good to carry a couple extra pills with you in case you end up crashing on someone's couch.

Here's an excerpt from a letter Sascha wrote to an 18-year old kid who'd just gotten out of the psych ward and was struggling to figure out what role he wanted drugs to play in his life:

"And this is the most important thing I'll tell you: **you need to get enough sleep**, okay? Even though that edge space of night and day is where most of the good stuff happens, you can't be there all the time. Not everyone can do what you do, but you gotta save all that ability for when you really need it. That's where the Zyprexa they're giving you comes in. If you want to get scientific about it, Zyprexa or olanzapine, dulls the dopamine receptors in your brain, keeps them from firing out of control, because people like us have too much too fast going on. We overheat and catch on fire. We see too much and take in too much until we're blind and burnt out. Zyprexa itself isn't evil. Eli Lilly, the company that makes it, definitely is evil, but the drugs are just tools. If you catch it early enough they say you can do the same thing with meditation and yoga and tai chi and herbs. But I know for myself that I can take all the valerian and skullcap and california poppy and kava kava and blue vervain I can stomach and I'm still clawing at the walls and wandering the late night streets. I take 2.5mgs of Zyprexa when I can't sleep sometimes and it knocks me on my ass. Which is just what I need periodically to get me back on track. Sweet sleep, brings me back down to earth speed. Which is really important to be able to do if you want to make your way around this world."

Paying attention to our sleep can help us learn our own cycles, and learn to control the extremes and take advantage of the creative energy of our manias and the depressive energy that draws us back into ourselves. The modern medical model sees our moods as dysfunctions, but those of us who know better see potential in our internal changes and sensitive chemistry. We just have to be more careful than other folks. **It's the responsibility that comes with having extra gifts.**

Dreams

There's something very strange about the fact that our culture doesn't take dreams more seriously. Dreams are full of clues if we allow ourselves to see them. All masked in layers of metaphor and symbol. Keep a pad and paper by your bed and write your dreams every night – just start with whatever little fragment comes out, it gets easier the more you do it. It's like exercising a muscle, you get more control after awhile. Dream journals are a whole other set of maps, maps to the underground unconscious each of us carries around with us. Sometimes dreams can even let us know where we are and where we might be going.

Food and Healing—the things Jacks wishes someone told them long ago…

There are so many things that can make us feel powerless, from the overwhelming amount of violence on the evening news to the way our families treat us. Being prone to extreme mood swings can make us feel totally trapped by our biochemistry in a way that is really hard to deal with. And we are almost always told that the doctor is the person with the power to fix it. When I first got out of the hospital I was told to call my shrink if I had any hint of "symptoms"— racing thoughts, a single night of sleeplessness, an overwhelming desire to flee. It made me fear myself. It made me panic that I was headed straight back to the hell of a total breakdown every time I laid down to sleep and saw an instant slideshow behind my closed eyes or felt a million ideas expanding in my brain.

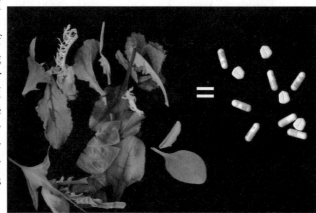

The way to deal with these behaviors never involved me and my decisions—it all came down to adjusting my medications. No one ever told me I would probably experience "symptoms"—to some degree—for the rest of my life. No one ever suggested that the cognitive and perceptual patterns of this "illness" are part of who I am, but that they could be kept to a level that didn't disrupt my daily existence. It seemed like I was supposed to expect and demand a state of complete normality, or else the drugs were failing. It seemed like all the power to manage my mind was in the hands of a man I saw for 30 minutes once a week.

Making deliberate choices about how we treat our bodies and minds can put the power back in our own hands. Deciding for ourselves what stability means, and how much our symptomatic behaviors need to be controlled, can put the power back in our hands. Telling ourselves, when we are experiencing a little depression or a day of particularly heightened vision, that it is not pathological and we are going to be fine once it passes, puts the power back in our own hands. Deciding for ourselves that a behavior feels like it's slipping past our control—that the thoughts are too fast or the desire to stay in bed too all-consuming—and helping ourselves, whether we do it by taking a pill, calling the doctor, or drinking a strong cup of chamomile tea, is putting the power back in our own hands.

For me, realizing that I could play a huge part in my own health by paying attention to what I eat has been incredibly empowering. It has not replaced traditional medicine entirely, but it has changed my life more than I can tell you. So here are a few of the things I've realized:

One of the most irresponsible things about Western medicine is that doctors don't ask you what you eat.

Think about how they're trained: they spend years in residency, working unbelievable hours, getting no sleep, drinking coffee and eating bad food. How are you supposed to learn to heal people when your very education requires treating your own body like crap? Is Western Medicine about health or is it about identifying symptoms off checklists and prescribing drugs?

I've seen a lot of doctors. I spent the first 21 years of my life with god-awful allergies, constant sinus infections, asthma, bronchitis, migraines, and incredibly volatile mood swings… The answer was *always* to put me on another medication: prednisone for the excruciating allergy attacks, a stronger antibiotic for the sinus infections that came afterwards, the latest expensive drug for migraines, a stronger inhaler for the asthma, a higher dose of Depakote for the craziness. No one ever asked why I got sick over and over and over. And no one ever thought about relating the illness in my body to the illness in my brain.

It wasn't until I found myself plagued with another round of unrelenting migraines that I looked past the Western Medical Establishment and opened up enough to investigate other forms of healing. I started reading a book called *Healing With Whole Foods; Asian Traditions and Modern Nutrition*, by Paul Pitchford. Exposing myself to different conceptions of health and treatment totally changed my life. I have discovered that I can actually be a physically strong person if I take good care of myself. I have hardly been sick since changing my diet in ways the author recommended. (But I have gone back on psych drugs. I think all the ways I deal with food have been instrumental in helping me get by on a very low dose, but at least for now, I find that I need pharmaceutical help too.)

So I'm going to share with you some of what I've learned. A suggestion: when I first got into this stuff I made this deal with myself that I would try these diet changes for 2 weeks and see if I felt a difference. I figured if I was willing to try taking a pill for 10 days, I might as well give kale a fair shot. After 2 weeks I felt better than I had in years. So if something sounds interesting to you, you have nothing to lose by jumping in and then doing some research of your own. There is SO much information out there if you start looking for it; this is only a tiny sliver. Please use what I've compiled as a starting point for your own investigations, and know that I'm not a professional, only a fellow traveler down this crooked path.

What is Manic Depression?

Interestingly, when you look into natural treatment of bipolar disorder you'll discover that most people advising treatments do see it as a condition with a biochemical component—but often they advocate treating it with food, enzymes, and herbs instead of pharmaceuticals. Allen Darmen **gives a clear explanation of a nutrient-based way of understanding manic depression on his very helpful website,** "Natural Treatment of Manic Depression Explained" (http://www.geocities.com/allen_dar/index.html):

> "Manic depression is a condition of biochemical imbalance in the biochemistry that all human beings are made out of, biochemicals with names such as neurotransmitters, hormones, and enzymes. The levels of neurotransmitters, hormones, and enzymes in the human body and brain are heavily dependent on the levels of essential nutrient precursor substances that these biochemicals are made out of, essential nutrient substances with names such as vitamins, minerals, amino acids. and essential fatty acids. In simple terms, correction of the condition of biochemical imbalance called manic depression involves correcting the levels of essential nutrient precursor substances in the human body, such that adequate and proper levels of neurotransmitters, hormones, and enzymes are maintained at all times. It also involves identifying and correcting all of the malabsorptive and allergic issues such that one's biochemistry became deficient such that a psychiatric diagnosis was the end result."

I recommend looking at his website for some very concrete suggestions about what kinds of food, enzymes, and vitamins are useful in treating bipolar. He is stridently anti-pharmaceutical, but his suggestions are very good. You'll definitely find some overlap between his piece and what I say below, but he gets specific about foods and things like stomach acid and proper bowel flora in a way I don't feel comfortable doing because I don't know enough.

Another excellent reference as far as specific foods go is the **"mood foods"** website: (**www.bipolarworld.net/Meds_Trt/Alt_trt/mood_food.htm**).

Yet another way to view manic depression is through the lens of Eastern Medicine. Chinese medicine looks at mental illness as an outgrowth of imbalances in various elements and energies, like fire and air, yin and yang, as well as a result of deficiencies in various organs, particularly the liver. I am not at all equipped to explain these ideas to you—but I want to suggest that there are different ways of understanding mental illness within different healing traditions. Again, I would recommend *Healing with Whole Foods* as a good place to start your own investigation of Eastern conceptions of health and practical steps to incorporate some of this wisdom into your daily life.

I'm going to start with what I do know from experience:

Three Meals A Day and Eating Breakfast

An easy place to start talking about correcting the kinds of nutrients in your body is to talk about how often you consume them. We've all heard that we should eat three meals a day but so many of us don't pay any attention. So often I was convinced I had way too much to *do* to cook 3 good meals… it was much more important to write furiously for nine hours and scarf a bowl of Cheerios around sunset than to eat something good for breakfast when it was still morning. But many bipolar people have hypoglycemic tendencies—if we don't eat regularly our blood sugar drops and it makes it hard to concentrate, easy to be irritable, and much more likely that we will have big ol' mood swings. If you eat a solid breakfast every day it's a lot easier to think, a lot easier to have control over what you eat later in the day—cause you're not running on empty—and it gives you a nice bit of routine and a sense that you're taking care of yourself. We need to stop, sit down, make contact with the physical world, and eat something humble like oatmeal. We get in trouble if we're up in our heads all day long. And eating regularly, whether that's 3 meals a day or always carrying an apple and half a sandwich in your bag in case you need it, makes the biggest difference in being able to function consistently and not hitting unnecessary crises of anger, angst, hysteria, depression, etc. And eating something that will give you sustainable energy—like proteins and complex carbohydrates—instead of quick fixes like bread products, sugary snacks, or junk food—makes a huge difference. Try it and you'll see.

Sugar

Eating Refined Sugar is Bad. It is especially bad for bipolar folks. Anyone you read for nutritional advice on healing bipolar will say this—it's pretty much unanimous. And most of us grow up eating tons of it. Sugar is in everything from apple pie to pasta sauce. Refined sugar (white sugar in particular) is a very concentrated substance, like cocaine, and it produces a drastic, immediate response in your body—spiking your blood sugar, which gives you temporary energy, and spiking the levels of serotonin in your brain, which temporarily elevates your mood—after which you experience a crash and want more sugar. For bipolar folks, who have these up and down patterns anyway, who tend towards hypoglycemia, and who tend to have very sensitive digestive systems, this can wreak havoc much more quickly than it might for our friends and family. And refined sugar has none of the minerals that help your body digest it like those found in foods with naturally occurring sugars (like whole grains, fruit, and sweet potatoes), so it weakens your digestive system and contributes exponentially to the development of yeast problems (candidiasis)—something so common in bipolar folks that many natural health practitioners think it can be **the cause** of bipolar disorder in people with susceptible systems. More about that later. But here are a few tips about getting off sugar: First off, do it gradually. Sugar is an addictive substance and your body will go through withdrawal. Have other foods around that you can eat when you're craving it, like carrots or apples. Often we reach for sugar when we really need protein to keep us going, but sugar is a much more immediate fix. If you eat regular meals, it will be easier to eat less sugar. You don't have to be perfect—but don't let sugar be a staple.

SAD: The Standard American Diet

So first let me confess: I am not a saint. Before I made all these changes I'm talking about I was a horrible eater. My favorite foods were fried chicken and blueberry donuts, and I consumed tons of processed food, tons and tons of sugar (I was totally addicted to Snickers, for one thing), lots of meat, lots of alcohol, lots of white bread and cookies, etc. etc. Then I found a page in *Healing with Whole Foods* that linked allergies, itchiness, headaches, sweets cravings, mood swings, yeast infections, general low immunity, a host of other symptoms, and **bipolar disorder** to candidiasis and I freaked out. Candidiasis is a condition of an overgrowth of yeast in the system. This develops when your body has trouble digesting the substances you put into it. Over time it causes a depressed immune system and the problems listed above. According to Paul Pitchford, the people most likely to develop these problems have probably grown up consuming large quantities of refined sugar, red meat, white flour, dairy, processed foods, and alcohol, and have often used large and repeated doses of antibiotics, all of which had been true for me. Now the obvious question is—don't so many Americans grow up like this? Yes they do (and compared to non-Western countries so many Americans have astounding rates of heart disease, diabetes, cancer, and obesity too…) but some of us are particularly sensitive, and it seems a lot of bipolar people (and this one for sure) can't tolerate this standard diet without having some serious problems.

Why these foods? To be very brief: white flour has been stripped of its whole-grain nutrition, and is a simple carbohydrate that immediately breaks down into sugar and is bad for the same reasons; processed foods lose most of their nutrition in the factory, and contain lots of artificial flavors, sugar and salt to replace the missing taste of food, as well as an assortment of chemicals that can mess with our brains; red meat is a very powerful food with a lot of fiery energy that over stimulates our system and we just don't need it in large quantities, and eating too much of it tends to make people crave more sugar; dairy is hard to digest and causes many people to form lots of mucus; alcohol is a sugar and taxes the hell out of your liver; antibiotics kill both the bad and good bacteria all throughout your body and mess up the balance

of necessary bacteria in your digestive tract that keep things chugging along, allowing yeast to multiply unchecked. Phew. So what do you eat instead? There are hundreds of books on this subject… but a few obvious answers: whole grains and other complex carbs instead of white flour; no meat or less intense meats like poultry and seafood; natural sugars instead of refined sugars; home-made food instead of processed food; LOTS OF VEGETABLES and a good chunk of vegetable protein (soy, beans, nuts, seeds, seaweeds/algae) instead of lots of simple carbohydrates. And try to keep yeasty foods (baked goods), chocolate, and caffeine to an occasional basis.

Food Allergies and Sensitivities

Bipolar people tend to have a lot of food allergies. The medical establishment rarely investigates things like this. Wheat and dairy are particularly frequent offenders. When I finally made a committed effort to cut these two out of my life, or limiting them to once or twice a week, it made a world of difference in my headaches, moods, and traditional allergy symptoms—runny nose, asthma, itching, etc. It's really amazing. You might have other allergies. Pay attention to when you start having problems and what you were eating in the days beforehand. For my father (who's also bipolar), it seems that he'll start having outbursts of irrational anger after eating chocolate. For me, if I eat white flour and cheese for several days in a row I start getting awful migraines and irritable moods. The best way to determine if you do have an allergy is to cut a suspected food out of your diet entirely for 2 weeks, and then gradually reintroduce it and see what your body does. If you do discover allergies, there are often alternative foods you can substitute—I can eat goat and sheep dairy, and do just fine with different kinds of flour like kamut, oat, and spelt, for example. Also, sometimes you can tolerate these foods in moderation. I can eat wheat and cow dairy once or twice a week and feel just fine, sometimes even a little more, but as soon as I start to eat them regularly I start to have problems. Also, if I've been really strong and stress-free dairy doesn't seem to bother me much at all, but I've been under a lot of stress, deprived of sleep, or depressed, I don't do as well. You get the idea.

Alcohol (is also a food substance)

It's obvious that alcohol's a drug and we're not supposed to abuse it. We all know and often ignore this. But it's also really hard on your body. It's a sugar. It interferes with the absorption of vitamins and minerals like calcium. It fills your liver with toxins. It's hard for many people to digest and can contribute greatly to yeast problems. It depresses your immune system. When you're drinking it can be much harder to control your food cravings (and how late you stay up, but I'm not trying to turn you into a nun.) If you cut back, your body will probably be very happy and your moods will probably be more stable. So this is a big one.

56

Things still go wrong sometimes. Our brains accelerate onto their own tracks and we might find ourselves heading back to a place we hoped we'd never have to revisit.

Written Plans

Just in case you end up in trouble again, it's a good idea to make some written plans that will leave clues for others in your life who want to help you. Getting things down on paper can even help you understand what's going on with yourself, and remind you later when you're losing track of what's real.

It's a good idea when you're in a relatively clear head space to sit down with the important people in your life and explain to them what you're going through in your various moods—and to clue them in, as much as you can, on what changes in your behavior they might notice that would help them recognize if you're starting to get manic or depressed and might need some help. It's an even better idea to write these things down.

"Before I moved back into my collective house in Oakland we all sat down as a group and read through my lists of warning signs and daily checklist. It was a little embarrassing at first, but it was also the first time I ever sat with a group of my friends and talked about mental health, mine or anyone else's, and it was such a powerful thing."-sascha

Part of sharing this information about yourself is agreeing that if your friends and family notice your behavior changing, they'll tell you and you'll try to trust their judgment. Come up with a written plan of what should happen—what you can do and what the people around you can do—if it seems like you're heading for trouble. It will give everyone something to refer back to when things get confusing. And if *you* write it then you theoretically don't end up having all your decisions made for you.

When Sascha got out of the halfway house they suggested the following "coping skills:"

let

"Let me out of here."

1. **Refer back to daily structure.**
2. **Take medication PRN's.**
3. **Call psychiatrist.**
4. **Call psychotherapist.**
5. **Go to emergency room.**
6. **Call 911.**

This list seems a little incomplete and drastic to us.

free

It doesn't suggest anything non-medical or intermediate, like talking to friends, doing yoga, cooking food, visiting old mentors, reading favorite books, immersing yourself in music, going for a swim, meditating, taking some herbs, going to church, whatever floats your boat... Though some of their advice does become necessary when things are really serious, this version of "coping" seems to reflect the priorities of a reductionist system that can't seem to imagine a form of health that doesn't rely solely on drugs, doctors, and the police. We can do better than that—but the first step is becoming very self-aware and getting to know your patterns intimately.

"What has worked best for me at the worst times is just to realize I am overstressed and I need at this time to slow down if I want to remain on track. I go against my own grain and force myself to connect to people, I walk, write, have a long hot shower....most importantly I rest... We have to realize our own limits and strengths... this is a real illness.. we need to take better care of ourselves like we would with any other disease.... we can transcend the cage..." -shine

What helps in the bad times?
Sweet advice from folks who've been there
(a discussion between members of the Icarus Project online forums)

what helps in the bad times? By: Icarus
hey all-- so sascha and i are putting together this reader, and we want to have a page or two on what helps us when we're in a bad place--being held, music, blue-green algae, whatever it is that people have found. here are a couple paragraphs i wrote:

Slight smile. Thich Nat Hanh and Ed Brown say to practice smiling. This can be so very hard. But sometimes when I am feeling particularly lost I will force the corners of my mouth up and the muscles will feel rusty, creaky, like the Tin Man's elbows after too much rain. But I will force them and if I am lucky I will remember a Buddha I saw at the Met once, a dark brown Buddha with the smallest, wisest smile. She was sitting cross-legged and when I looked at her I could tell that she was sitting with everything, waiting it all out and smiling over some inner mystery. I could tell she was kind and when I think of her I remember about kindness and about sitting cross-legged myself with an achy back trying to learn quiet and compassion in my muscles, and bones, where it might stick. If I am lucky the smile feels less forced by now and I remember something like the way the reeds rose up out of the pond by the bench where I would sit in the sunlight and feel the slightest hint of grace unfolding in my belly.

Books help. Food helps. Making myself get out of bed and cook something reminds me that I am capable of doing this life thing. The smell of garlic frying. The slippery tendencies of onions. When I eat I feel glad, for a little while at least, that I am actually taking care of myself. When I can't take care of myself and someone else cooks for me it helps more than you could ever imagine. It is sort of like being held.

animals   By: Anon
When my inner world sucks and I feel like cringing up and dying - I am removed from those feelings for a brief and shining moment when I can snuggle up with the warm, purring presence of one of my cats. Animals are great!

doing nothing by: dianalupi
funny that jacks mentioned blue green algae. I raved about that body- fuel one day on a long hike together. Funny that. Even that one comes in and out. Sometimes crave it and sometimes just don't want it. Cycles. Change. Anitcha....a beautiful word I learned recently in the Vipassana meditation tradition which means "change". The meditators come back to that word as their ass aches or the terror of quiet and mind scramble is assaulting. Anitcha. This too shall pass.

Anyway, the first thing that came to my mind on this question was doing nothing. Actually, more specifically, laying down and doing nothing. Might seem contra-indicated sometimes in depressed state, etc.....For me, sometimes, this is the moment of, " I feel like crap in one way or another and I don't have to DO anything about it necessarily." Don't have to do yoga or hike or eat or call a friend, etc. Sometimes I feel the wisdom of my body knows how to move things through energetically WAAAAAY better than some of these awesome pro-active resources I have and use. Sometimes just laying down and dozing into half awake state or wide awake or asleep....sometimes that feels like I'm giving my system the respect to get out of the way and allow "it" , me, to re-adjust on it's (my) own a bit,..........sometimes a little involuntary shaking does happen literally. Like my system is wiggling around some of the stuck or the hype and I just can watch. I can receive that help. That innate knowledge of me that I don't know, as yet, in my conscious mind. Waiting out the Anitcha. Doing absolutely nothing and understanding there's always something going on, we're never "doing nothing". Not feeling guilty about it or worried I'm so depressed, blah blah blah. Just lay on down. Allow the shift.

the movies, museums   By: eduardo
If I had more money I would just go to the movies all the time when depressed. Or at least rent piles of videos. The difficulty being that if I am REALLY down, I can't move myself out the door to the movie theater. But the basic function of cinema, entertainment, is a powerful drug. And it sure does take my mind off myself. museums are a GREAT way to kill depression and also fantastic for absorbing manic energy. you can rush around as fast as you want or as slow, and you can talk to yourself and comment

on the art or the idiots in your way, you can go shopping for postcards at the end to satisfy that little acquisitive compulsion, you can flip through all their books in the bookstore, etc.

(untitled) By: Permafrost

the random kitten generator (do a google search). needs no explanation- should be prescribed if one cannot actually take care of a real one.

Refusing to watch the news, read the newspaper or otherwise refusing to get involved with any abstract distant horrors or tragedies- there's no need to borrow misery at this point, seek out comedies and happy endings like the strong necessary medicine they are. Raising Arizona or Moonlighting, don't ask me why but Nicholas Cage figures largely in this thing. OR if you're secretly a gay man like I am, go rent Kiss Me Kate, or anything involving Cole Porter or Busby Berkely or Carmen Miranda. Or listen to something that underpins the sadness with company- I know it's goofy but I love the Smiths and the Cure for times like these- they can remind you of the bittersweetness and symmetry of it all, any voluptuary, wistful, longing thing.

being taken care of by someone loving, in a slightly regressive way for a little while (which has only happened to me once but i think about it wistfully) or being looked in on, invasively if necessary (we're worried about you and we came even though you said not to). having someone that loves you drag your ass out of bed in a very firm manner and make you accompany them to some activity that will engage you completely for a while (exercise teaching a class etc.)- and hopefully doing this every day, when you can't do it for yourself- until you're well enough to be trusted to keep up the routine. Just any way really someone can help you enforce a routine initially if you've already fallen so far down, and keep up with you and at you until it's firmly established.

Having someone love you unconditionally and not seek to "cheer you up", or offer endless advice about what else you can do (implying that somehow you haven't really been trying) when you're there (depression feels like a hinterland of awareness, so often when I'm not there i refer to it as something far away) but just be willing to accompany and witness- so you're not alone at the outer reaches- someone anchoring you to the fact, even if abstract at the time, that life may possibly be sometime in the future, a thing worth fighting for, that they'll be waiting for you and will help you get back to land.

That they witness and acknowledge your struggle and bravery-
-that's a big one.

Often some professional does a history or intake and after I've regurgitated in a quavery robot monotone what the recent past "stressors" have been- I'm always caught off guard if they look at me and they mean it and they say- "it's been hard hasn't it, and you've been so brave" as opposed to duly noting it all down without comment. OR that someone sees the pain and knows it the way you do (you know a brother or sister- one of the mood-struggling many) and share whatever temporary grace they have, with you, lend it to you for a little while and assure you, stating with the kind of authority that only a survivor can summon, that they've been where you are, that there IS a way back, and that where you are IS a real place and, maybe, even, a necessary place to be sometimes.

Unexpected gifts, and food, thoughtfully prepared. Any type of quasi-maternal ministering- ESPECIALLY if you can't reciprocate- or, conversely, forcing yourself to write letters of gratitude when envious or bitter, or, attempting to conjure a mental inner avatar of some figure that's comforted you in the past and feeling all new age and stupid but thinking hard about it anyways, projecting that warmth at yourself.

but now I'm getting redundant - just warmth and love- whether or not you can acknowledge it or return it at the time- much like the TV show coma victim- to be spoken to in warm, loving, patient tones, even if, in many ways you are truly absent. to have your people ignore all evidence to the contrary (preemptive strike isolation or withdrawal) and still treat you like you are there and you can hear them and that they are waiting for you- patiently holding your place.

"Loose Associations" and Forecasting Dreams
Keeping Track of Your Warning Signs

Part of taking care of yourself is learning to recognize the signs that indicate you're heading into dangerous territory. When Sascha got let out of the last halfway house, he was sent into the world with a list of warning symptoms to watch out for and a list of "coping skills" to help deal with them. While we think this is a good idea, we don't think they did the best job identifying symptoms or suggesting creative ways to handle them. So we're going to share their list first, and then give you a list we brainstormed based on our observations of ourselves over the years. We encourage you to make your own and share it with the people in your life.

Mild
Thoughts crowding head
Feeling a need to go faster
Calling in sick to work
Leaving town
Not following through daily routine; missing any component of daily routine
Sleeping through alarm clock
Feelings of euphoria
Feelings of depression

Moderate
Missing a dose of medication
Traveling without adequate plans for sleeping arrangements etc.
Impulsive behavior
Feeling an urgent need to do something
Sleeping all day
Not being able to sit still
Taking on too many projects
Difficulty concentrating

Severe
Not sleeping
Racing thoughts
Decreasing medications without consulting psychiatrist
Quitting job without significant planning
Delusions
Loose associations (!!?!!)
Suicidal ideation
Stopping medications

We've arranged our list with manic symptoms on the left and depressive symptoms on the right. Obviously not all of these hold for everyone, and some don't always indicate a problem—as Sascha has pointed out, some people are bad about remembering to pay their bills all the time, not just when they're "symptomatic," for example.

Getting Manic...?

--forecasting dreams and other ESP stuff (knowing who's on the phone, when things are going to happen, what someone's going to say etc.)

--start waking up earlier and earlier, or staying up later and later

--increased desire to flee/travel/adventure!!!

--food—think about eating less often, or eat voraciously but stay skinny

--seems less and less important to take care of practical things like cleaning room/bills/dishes. very easy to overlook completely—not even see the bag of month-old food rotting on the floor or the dishes in the sink.

--driving more aggressively/scattered/miss exits/don't pay attention as much

--recruit more people into my life. promise to hang out with everybody. much easier to make friends.

--promise to take lots of things on—projects, jobs, classes, meetings

--start scheduling almost every hour of my day full of plans

--It's hard to watch TV and pay lots of attention to the storylines, but TV is the most fascinating thing in the world from an anthropological point of view. Everything is so interesting to analyze.

--Become convinced I'm falling in love with people or just develop intense, all-consuming crushes. Start getting much more interested in sex and it seems easier to come by, more reasonable to have casually.

--Vision/Perception changes—everything becomes more vivid, more clear, often more beautiful and meaningful, I start seeing patterns everywhere and notice everything.

Getting Depressed...?

--My intuition is off— I misjudge people's intentions and have lots of bad hunches. Assume everyone's thinking about me and noticing how awful I am.

--I start wanting to sleep around 4 in the afternoon

--it's getting harder to see anything good anywhere

--start disliking how I look: feel fat, or ugly, or hate all my clothes

--crave sugar constantly. if I'm getting especially ornery I start wanting to binge on tequila and whiskey.

--desire to flee/need to change my job/house/friends/location/haircut

--seems like it requires so much energy to take care of practical things like cleaning room/bills/dishes

--seems unreasonably hard to get out of bed or out of the house

--can't concentrate

--doing anything that involves multiple tasks seems so incredibly complicated—requires way too much energy

--spending too much time on internet

--canceling all my appointments with people

--TV seems overwhelmingly awful and the newspaper is unbearably distressing. Advertisements are obviously the devil's work.

--Start doubting my relationships. If I'm with someone I start thinking we don't fit and should probably just break up. If I'm interested in someone I'm sure they don't like me.

--Everything seems flat and dull and I notice all the rats in the alleys instead of the birds in the sky.

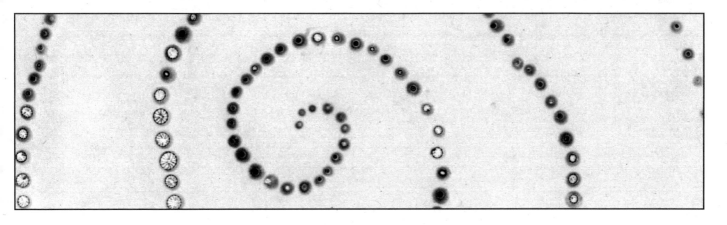

Whether or not people diagnosed with bipolar disorder can keep themselves steady without taking psych drugs is a highly disputed question. The medical establishment's line on the dilemma is clear; studies prove bipolar people should take meds for the rest of their lives. This can be really hard to swallow. It seems like some of us do manage to find non-pharmaceutical methods of coping; we might pay very close attention to our nutrition, exercise constantly, and/or develop a consistent meditation practice, or we might turn to alternative practitioners for treatments like acupuncture and herbs. Some try these treatments and find that they aren't sufficient by themselves, but are immensely helpful in addition to psychiatric treatment. The vast majority of us end up trying pharmaceuticals at some point—some of us stay on them for decades, some of us go off them after a few months. Some of us have trouble with side-effects and feel dampened; some of us are unequivocally sure that they infinitely improve the quality of our lives. Because the debate on what works best has so many sides, we want to let the voices of the amazing members of our website speak to you about their experiences so you can decide what makes sense for yourself.

"I used to be a hardcore nature-girl, never considered medications. I've suffered a long time undiagnosed and self-berating for "not getting my shit together" and being so devastated when a hypomanic stage would end right when I thought I was all "healed" and "gonna finally be alright." Whatever your spiritual bent, these days I simply refer to the Herbalists as the Forest Healers and the scientists whipping up my little blue Wellbutrins as the Merlins. It's all magic to me and my life has vastly improved since opening my horizons to all the options available. Absolutely anything can be over used or under used, over prescribed, under prescribed, over eaten, under eaten. Takes a lot of patience to find the right stuff for each one of us. And then the openness and flexibility to realize once we find some good help, our needs may change." –dianalupi

One of the hardest things about deciding whether or not to take drugs is the criticism we impose on ourselves and the judgments we fear from others. People who are deciding whether to take or reject drugs are trying to understand how to heal themselves; they are neither weak for "giving in" and taking drugs nor stupid and irrational for questioning them.

"whatever helps you feel better- i'll probably say that so many times i should take the time to learn how to program a shortcut key for it- I couldn't tolerate meds well in the past and am seeking and investigating alternatives- but whatever helps you live and alleviates the suffering- at a certain point whether it comes out of a brown plastic vial or someone's mouth or off a tree- you're worth it - your happiness is probably worth some risk, yes?"-permafrost

Whether the drugs are an evil form of mind control, divine intercession, or something in between is not a simple question to answer. We all experience them differently.

"I think that the debate on this will rage forever and ever. It does inside me all the time. I personally don't take pharmaceuticals, although I can say they have saved my life in the past. I just don't like who I am when I am on them. It's like a different kind of depression for me, like I'm trying to kill a part of myself, cutting off an arm or something. I have been on every kind of med imaginable, and a few that I don't even know about from when I was hospitalized. I don't know if it is completely the best decision for me, but it's the decision I've made and I'm working super hard on maintaining my sanity herbally and through processing and dealing with things with a tight knit group of folks that I live with."-jennyrogue

For those of us who can tolerate them, the drugs can retrieve the outside world from its hiding spot behind the machinations of our minds.

"I had so much rage that the real me, the one I liked and understood, had been swallowed up by this swirling gray mess that wouldn't lift no matter what I did, and I wanted her back.... But she came back. Each time, it's seemed like forever. Like unending awfulness. But at some point I realized it had ended. The drugs were, to say the very least, an enormous relief. After a few weeks, I could read again. The incessant despair and circular racing of my brain like a hamster on a wheel to nowhere slowed, and eventually leveled out. There was a day when the sunrise was beautiful and gentle and I could sit through the whole thing without fidgeting. A day when I could be patient. A day when there were no voices in my head. When a good apple tasted good. When I understood how to be human again. And gradually there were more of those days, and now I feel more like myself than I have in years."-a

Yet it seems to some of us that the drugs are prescribed for all the wrong reasons, and create as many problems as they address.

"I resented being sent to counselors because I knew too many "punks" institutionalized and medicated for what I thought of as normal teenage rebellions and creativity. I saw myself as just another example of such -- but too well-adjusted and eloquent to be caught in that trap for long. The sadnesses I dealt with I saw as normal (boyfriend break-ups and a truly fucked home-life). When I became morbid and suicidal out of the blue during freshman year in college, I was worried and an appointment was made with a psychiatrist. He took a quick history and sent me back to college with a script for Prozac, which I took for 3 days. By the 3rd night I was shaking with crying jags and obsessive morbid

thought loops like a really bad acid trip come down. I ran to my friend's house in the middle of the night and never saw a doctor again. I'd always been incredibly suspicious of pharmaceutical companies in general and was really frightened by the pervasive use of poorly understood and relatively new molecules."-w

It is an almost indescribable experience to watch the workings of our minds change as we introduce new chemicals into our bodies. Sometimes we can think more clearly and consistently then we ever thought possible. Sometimes we feel totally irrational and see the strangest things in our heads. The permutations are truly bizarre.

"Since starting lamictal (and trazodone some days to help me sleep), I've noticed that sometimes I'm a little tired and my mind "goes to sleep" for a few moments (or half asleep), at which point I have little dream fragments. And I tell you honestly, it's seeing the machinery of my cognition be partially disassembled: certain wheels are spinning, but they aren't connected the way they were. It's literally like that. I have spatial models spinning in my head that normally would be a part of a larger mental machine, but it's like I've taken the motor out or disconnected some belts and the motor is just spinning on its own. It's accompanied by a dullness and mild confusion."-NG

One of the biggest deterrents to taking drugs, or to remaining on them indefinitely, is the potential for serious side effects. This can be particularly tricky for women who want to get pregnant—do you stay on the drugs and risk birth defects, or do you go off them and risk impossible mood swings?

"...my partner and i really want to have kids, and i want to be the one to be pregnant. i'm on lithium and zyprexa, neither of which are approved for pregnancy. my doctor wants me to quit lithium and stay on zyprexa. anyone have thoughts about that? been there? alternatives?" –daniellefrances

The answers vary because we do not all have the same chemistry. If you look at pharmacology textbooks and the like, you'll discover that they're very formulaic when it comes to prescribing medicine: the usual combo is a mood stabilizer + an antidepressant, with only a few variations.

"Patience is key when looking for the right drugs and the right person who actually bothers to keep up on the current research and actually bothers to listen to you as an individual, not a "typical bi-polar" which, as we know from our wide and varied stories, there is no such thing… I tried my 10th shrink and he listened and recognized my particular life-story/ patterns…Started me on Wellbutrin which some psychiatrists would never do because if you've ever had a manic episode, they go straight to the mood-stabilizers which can be such DOWNERS for those of us already usually in a down. Wellbutrin doesn't work on serotonin but the other neuro transmitter, dopamine. Less likely to put someone in mania........within a half hour of popping this thing I didn't feel like I wanted to die for the first time in months. Just like that. Wow. What we ended up with was Wellbutrin and Ritalin during the day for depression and focus. AND, very important, Klonopin at night for relaxation and sleep. So as an alternate story to some of those on here who talk of taking Zyprexa or others to sleep only in manic times, I'm someone who, for the moment takes all three of these as my daily diet and, let me tell you, my metabolism and problems with digestion and eating disorders quieted, my ability to focus, function........amazing how physiological it all really is."-dianalupi

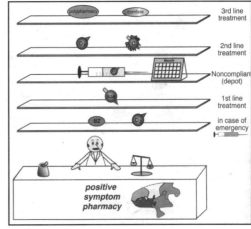

The Lithium Debates
Another dialogue from the members of the Icarus Project Website

What About Lithium? By: Luckylilly

Does lithium actually slow down the insidious constant rambling in your mind? For example I'm a musician and I just can't keep up with all the ideas, I feel like I open a closet door and either I'm buried alive with a thousand ideas I can't swim my way out of or I open the door a month later and the skeleton is staring back telling me the joke again, you know, the one about the stupid piece of sh*t lazy artist that thought she was gifted enough to create something worthwhile, something more than mediocre.

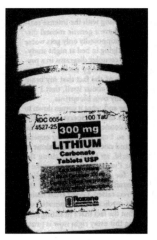

Does lithium actually make it so that when I open the door there may be 10 or so useful creative ideas and breathing room to focus on them and actually finish projects? I have so many unfinished songs but can't seem to pick and choose and finish, and then I'd rather be writing new stuff, there's just too MUCH it's totally, utterly overwhelming and it seems like when I'm motivated (hypomanic) I get so overexcited I can't STAND it I feel like screaming I'm SO FAR BEHIND and everything could be SO AMAZING if I could just FOCUS and STAY THAT WAY for a LONG ENOUGH and never burn out or get sick or have interruptions like work, friends, food, sleep, and of course those nasty depressions inevitable as breathing in is to breathing out (except breathing out lasts months longer than it should).

Lithium--love it, curse it, take it, abhor it?   By: Icarus
I'm really curious to know what people out there think about Lithium. I swore up and down for years I would never take it, refused it, tried everything else, went off drugs altogether and tried eating good food and doing yoga, ended up back on other drugs, met people who took Lithium and liked it but still refused to try it, but finally last month found myself pudging up like a blowfish, feeling like a total zombie on Zyprexa, and the other drugs didn't do shit, So I finally agreed to try lithium... And I feel 6000 times better, much to my surprise. So I want to know what other people think about the stuff, especially people who've been on it long-term.

Lithium   By: maya7maya
I hated taking lithium or any pills forever. My body weight made it hard to keep me level and not get toxic. Being an ultra rapid cycling bipolar with mixed states, we tried everything and most of it made me feel like a zombie. I just came through another severe triggering jolt that increased my cycling at least 10 fold. I moved back to where my initial psychiatrist was; ended up hospitalized for suicide watch. He took me off all my meds and restarted me on lithium or something for sleep, thyroid medication which is good for rapid cycling and Lamictal for the mixed states and depression. I feel great. So much fear from so many misses by doctors for years and years. Lithium has its side effects but nothing like Depakote, Zyprexa or this new Abilify. I don't want to be a zombie but I don't want to be stuck in my surreal world either. Thanks for letting me share.

Lithobid   By: TL Chenhall
Personally, I don't have the budget for the amount of toilet paper demanded by Lithium.
I imagine that because lithium is an older medication, it is less refined. Less specific to the target. Now take a new medication like Abilify, which I was on for about a month. Highly refined. The pills are tiny, and effect a very specific part of the brain. I found myself unable to stop moving and barely able to sit still long enough to sleep. They should just print 'HELL' on these little yellow bastards.
Anyway, when I was on Lithium, my visualizing faculty accelerated greatly. Especially as I was going to sleep, I would see a rapid slide-show of shifting forms. However, in keeping with the textbook, I found my creative output stifled. (Lithium interferes with Thyroid function.) I'm not saying Zyprexa is right for everyone, but for me, the side effects (eating and sleeping more than usual) are both less abrasive than Lithium.

"there I go again shaking but I ain't got the chills..." By: scatter

(That was a line from a Clash song off the album London Calling.) That's about where my life was at two years ago when I was living in a halfway house and my body was getting used to the new foreign substance I was putting in it everyday. I called it the "lithium shakes", I was pretty miserable. Up until they locked me up and started force-feeding it to me with a colorful array of other moodstabilizers/antipsychotics/ antidepressants, I had never heard of the drug. I never would have guessed that these tiny little pills would end up playing such an important role in my life. This coming January it'll be three years I've been on the stuff, and my life has changed so dramatically in really good ways.

We all react to the world and to the various substances we put in our bodies differently, but I don't believe for a second that lithium has stunted my creativity. I'm more creative than I've ever been. And I actually finish things I start these days!

But we'll see. The flipside is that I hate being dependent on the medical establishment for my stability. I don't trust the corporate drug companies for a second. Who knows what life is going to look like for me or anyone else in ten years, in twenty years? The whole social/economic system we live under is held together by an emotionally deadening consumer culture that is going to end up destroying us in really ugly and ironic ways unless we figure out better models of living our lives. So we have a lot of work to do. At the moment though, while it's obviously walking a sketchy line, I'm very happy for my Medicaid card and my little pills.

Lithium Frankenstein experience By: dianalupi

So, I was really stoked on trying lithium because it's pretty much just a mineral salt. Felt it to be the most simple and "natural" thing to take, etc etc blah blah. Well, I'm some kinda mix of bi-polar two, mixed-states, cyclothymia. The depression is more of a presence than the "highness" in whatever degree it comes, hyper or hypo or pain in the ass enthusiastic and lots of energy before the "fall" comes. Bottom line on my two cents on this subject: lithium was not a match for me. Felt like leaden feet/body Frankenstein monster on the lowest of low doses. **I wanted everything to be groovy and "happy ending" with lithium like Patty Duke in her autobiography. Well, I was a bit bitter and back to the drawing board.**

Lithium has too many side effects   by: nova

Lithium did not work for me. Neither did Tegretol (allergic reaction, face and tongue turned numb), Lamictal (wired me into a breakdown), Depakote (worked except for hair loss) Neurontin (wired me, gnashing teeth), Zyprexa (change in senses).... I am on Topamax, which is actually working incredibly for me. But have only been on it for two months. Side effects almost non-existent. I feel totally like myself. A calm and happy and rational version of myself, that is. :) And for the record, I also do yoga, am vegan/ vegetarian, get therapy and take naturopathic medicines. And try massage and acupuncture when money comes in. But meds are definitely a necessity.

What is working for me... by: Madliberator

After I got out of the hospital the last time around, I saw my regular psychiatrist. She put me on seroquel and, for the first time, Lithium. And in a few months, I felt close to normal. I have been pretty consistent with those meds since then. Last winter I went into the hospital cause I was a little suicidal, and a close friend insisted, but I haven't had a psychotic episode since march 2002. I averaged one every 8 months or so in the ten years previous.

I still felt really conflicted about taking meds...mostly cause of my views about post-industrial society, but had made a promise to myself to stick with it for a year, to see if it would keep me from having an episode. Notwithstanding depression, it did. I was angry that it worked, like, that somehow meant something was wrong with me, like I was "sick" or something. When I saw Sascha's Bipolar World article, I began to think about that middle ground, that I could reconcile my beliefs about psychiatry and society with the fact that lithium frees me from the fear of psychosis, without debilitating me.

Lithium works for me. Of course, it won't work for everyone, and I am always looking for a natural method that works. Still, as critical as I feel of psychiatric drugs, I know that for some, sometimes, they provide the chance for a better life...

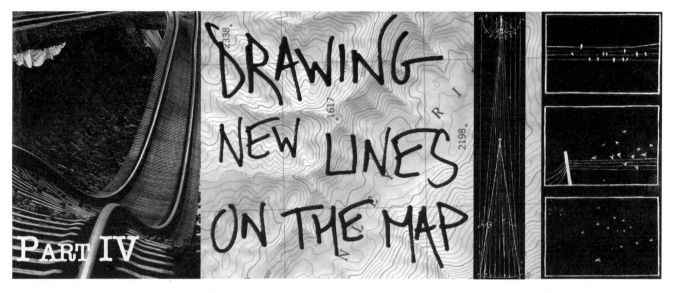

DRAWING NEW LINES ON THE MAP

PART IV

We are the people who should have the power to say who we are and of what we are capable. We are people with a dangerous gift that sometimes grants us the vision to see new possibilites and offers the potential of drawing new lines on the map. Drawing new lines on the map requires being critical of the ones that have already been set down—while being realistic about what can and cannot be changed. Drawing new lines on the map requires allowing ourselves free access to our imaginations. It requires the courage to resist authority—and ultimately, the solidarity to do it well.

Downtown Seattle Late November 1999

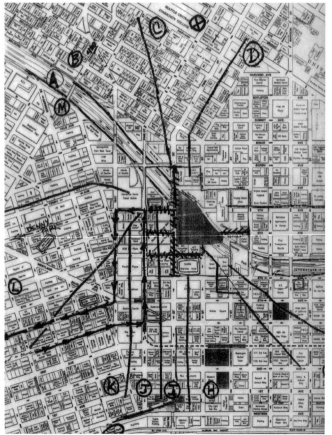

"I'm just trying to come to terms with what I am, who I am... in an honest fashion that isn't obscured by denial of this difficult electricity in my personality nor by monstrous self-effacement. I want to face down the challenges that I now know I must. I want to accept having to take a pill every day for the rest of my life--accept it so that I am not pushing against the walls that seem to have suddenly sprung up around me. I'm starting to realize that these walls have always been there... they're more like moats, really, and I have fallen into them time and again. Touching upon the artistic streak, the creativity, the shimmering treasure of human genius documented in bipolar people helps me step up from the despondency and despair of feeling I am a broken human being. It helps me recognize that I am not surrounded by chasms of impossibility on all sides. Some moats and chasms are there, but other ways are open. I see myself more clearly than I ever have before. I'm still the most challenging puzzle I've ever faced, but now the sun has risen and I'm rubbing my eyes awake. I've got a rudimentary map and I'm being honest about the terrain and I'm being honest about what I've got in my bag." -NG

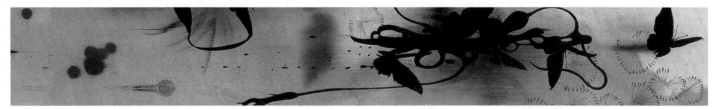

There are so many lenses through which we can look at the experiences that get labeled mental illness; one of the more imaginative is shamanism*. Shamanism is a tradition found in virtually every primitive society, in every forgotten corner of the world. According to Alberto Villoldo and Erik Jendresen, the authors of *Four Winds: A Shaman□s Odyssey into the Amazon*, the shaman

"… was a 'person of knowledge,' a 'man or woman of vision,' a mediator between the natural and supernatural forces of nature. Because these were the forces that the shaman held responsible for health and disease, the shaman was a healer." (p.13)

Shamans are people who seem to contact spirits and have access to different versions of reality than the ones most people inhabit. In traditional cultures this ability was seen as a gift, and it was considered sacred. In modern cultures it is seen as a pathology, and labeled psychotic. In most non-Western cultures, there is not even a word for what we call manic depression. This label is a small box that doesn't fit all of us, and the world around it is so much bigger and more complicated than what it can describe.

"i insist that i am not flawed. i am a shaman without mentor or training, without a spiritual safety net, changing as i am moved by the spirit of life that connects me to the rest of the world. i move to my own inner orders. my chemistry is balanced, however it may differ from the mythical Norm. i don't believe in Norm. i believe in biodiversity. including that which may be found in the biochemistry of people.
a really twisted, deformed duckling? or an adolescent swan? whose call is that to make? who is permitted to define what evolution did and did not intend?"-fireweed

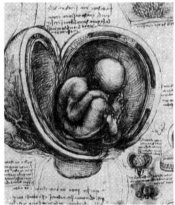

It's possible the powers of the shaman could be intensely useful to modern civilization.

It's possible they offer a hope of becoming something more than we are—or perhaps it is a hope of emerging into clarity and seeing our world exactly as it is, in all its dimensions.

But these powers don't have a place into the framework we've constructed. We don't know how to hone, rather than fear, the exceptional abilities of our minds, as becomes obvious in the following dialogue from *Four Winds* between an American psychologist and a Peruvian professor of philosophy.

"'The Western world,' he said, 'the "civilized" nations, what is called the "first world" cultures rule the Earth by right of their economic and military strength. And the philosophical foundation of the Western culture is based on a religion that teaches of the fall from grace, original sin, and the exodus from the Garden of Eden. This concept is fundamental to the mythology of the West, and it represents Nature as hostile and man as corrupt.'

---

* *Since the writing of this piece we have become familiar with the complexities of taking a word like shaman from one corner of the world and applying it universally to indigenous healers and guides from many different traditions. We're also aware of the ways that westerners often harm other cultures by adopting their practices and profiting from them. In a context of cultural appropriation and neocolonialism, it's complicated for Westerners to call ourselves shamans. Nonetheless, we still find this language useful if understood as a shorthand for wounded healers with magical or spiritual inclinations, and so many readers of Navigating the Space have found these articles helpful that we have decided to include them in their original forms. We hope these essays can spark discussions that include an analysis of the power dynamics involved when Western peoples who have lost our own indigenous practices seek authentic spiritual connection in the practices of the peoples we have colonized.*

'I dipped my collapsible camping cup into the stream and offered it to him.

'Adam and Eve eat of the fruit of the tree of knowledge of good and bad,' he said. He took a drink and handed back the cup. 'And God said: "Cursed is the ground on your account. In the sweat of your face you will eat bread until you return to the ground, for out of it you were taken. For dust you are and to dust you will return."

'And so,' I quoted, ' "he drove them out and posted at the east of the Garden of Eden the cherubs and the flaming blade of a sword to guard the way to the tree of life." '

It is such a peculiar myth,' he said, '**The emphasis is not man's relationship to his environment, to Nature, to the Garden , but man's relationship to himself as an outcast, fending for himself, become self-conscious in a hostile world.** The Westerner has accepted this tradition, has promoted this concept through art and literature and philosophy. Indeed, is has become ingrained and second nature, has it not?'

'I suppose it has,' I agreed. 'You can live your entire life in a city, for instance. It provides shelter, a controlled environment, and acts as a buffer between the individual and Nature. Even foods in the supermarket are treated before they are consumed, either artificially ripened, colored, or preserved, then packaged for consumption.'

'So the Westerner,' he said, 'the outcast from the Garden, has turned inward, and, it is interesting that within such a culture, when the individuals experience a psychological crisis of some sort, a psychotic or neurotic episode, they will turn to religion or the psychiatrist or medication instead of to Nature to become well again. To become normal. Is this not so?' … 'But,' he continued, '**you end up with an entirely different focus when the tradition of a culture is not founded on the fall from grace, where man was never banned from the Garden of Eden and lives close to Nature and Nature is a manifestation of the Divine.**

In those cultures a psychotic break or a schizophrenic episode is magical. The unconscious mind opens up, and, if the person is young, he or she is encouraged to dive into it, not pull back from the brink. They fall into their unconscious, into the realm of pure imagination , the realm of Jung's archetypes, into a world of spirit. They are allowed to experience other realms of their own minds and they are changed as a result. In many primitive cultures, they become the medicine people. They have experienced the Divine.'

'**I propose nothing of the kind. It would be dangerous to promote such incidents within your culture, because your mythology is based on thousands of years of tradition that such episodes are not normal, are unnatural, are unhealthy. I am merely pointing out a difference. In primitive cultures the opening of the unconscious is a blessing. It is unusual, yes. But not unnatural. These are children of the Earth, the Garden, living in Nature, not banished from it. In such a culture everything is of Nature. Natural. Even a psychotic episode. It is safe, especially when guided by one who has had a similar experience.**'

'Madness is a social distinction?' I said.

'Precisely.' " (pp. 88-90)

THE WESTERN PARADIGM OF MADNESS IS NEATLY DEFINED AND CATEGORIZED IN NUMBERED CODES AND 1000 PAGE DOCUMENTS BY HUGE ORGANIZATIONS WITH ACRONYMS AND LOBBIES IN CONGRESS, BUT IT DOESN'T TAKE ORGANIZATIONS AND STRUCTURES LIKE ITSELF INTO ACCOUNT WHEN DECIDING WHO'S MAD. IT LOOKS AT PEOPLE LIKE YOU AND I. AS DAVID OAKS, THE PRESIDENT OF MINDFREEDOM, HAS OBSERVED.

"**There are different types of madness. Some can cost you a job and break a window and screw things up. Others can get you a job as President of the USA. But mad we all are. And that should mean HUMILITY… humility on how we treat each other, and humility on how we treat the Earth. And it should mean society running to the doors of people labeled "seriously mentally ill" who have fully recovered to find out HOW THEY DID IT because, the fact is, those are the lessons the Earth needs desperately right now.**"

It's striking how much overlap there is between the tendencies and behaviors our society attributes to the "seriously mentally ill" and the tendencies and behaviors a shamanic culture views as prerequisite for someone to undergo the initiation into shamanic practice. Descriptions of the transition period itself ring a remarkable number of bells for many of us who've undergone the process of descending from intensely visionary manias and psychoses into the figurative death of depression, and then emerging to reconstruct ourselves as someone who has walked through the fire and come back to the other side.

The shamanic corollary of this process is elegantly articulated in the book *Food of the Gods: The Search For the Original Tree of Knowledge*, by Terence McKenna:

"The ecstatic part of the shaman's initiation is….dependent on a certain receptivity to states of trance and ecstasy on the part of the novice; he may be moody, somewhat frail and sickly, predisposed to solitude, and may perhaps have fits of epilepsy or catatonia, or some other psychological aberrance (though not always as some writers on the subject have asserted). In any case, his psychological predisposition to ecstasy forms only the starting point for his initiation: the novice, after a history of psychosomatic illness or psychological aberration that may be more or less intense, will at last begin to undergo initiatory sickness and trances; he will lie as though dead or in deep trance for days on end. During this time, he is approached in dreams by his helping spirits, and may receive instruction from them. Invariably during this prolonged trance the novice will undergo an episode of mystical death and resurrection; he may see himself reduced to a skeleton and then clothed with new flesh; or he may see himself boiled in a cauldron, devoured by the spirits, and then made whole again; or he may imagine himself being operated upon by the spirits, his organs removed and replaced with "magical stones" and then sewn up again.

In short, the shaman is transformed from a profane into a sacred state of being. Not only has he effected his own cure through this mystical transmutation, he is now invested with the power of the sacred, and hence can cure others as well. It is of the first order of importance to remember this, that the shaman is more than merely a sick man, or a madman; he is a sick man who has healed himself, who is cured, and who must shamanize in order to remain cured." (p. 5)

What does it mean to shamanize in order to remain cured? Is it possible that sharing what we've been through, all we've seen and all we've learned, might open doors in a society that is rapidly constructing walls around possibility at every bend? Is it possible that the very pieces of ourselves that get labeled pathological could also be like keys in the dark, their edges barely glowing, like silver question marks too easy to overlook? After all, would I be making the imaginative leaps necessary to write this piece you're reading if my mind wasn't prone to unifying visions, dendritic and unusual connections across vast swaths of thought, and the "delusions of grandeur" that get labeled symptomatic of disease but also allow me to have a wide open vision that reconsiders the role madness can play in our culture and imagines big possibilities?

What do the ravings of a madman look like? Are they always incoherent nonsense with little relationship to reality? Or is there a brilliance sometimes, an ability to see phenomena as part of larger systems, to recombine the elements of daily existence through linguistic tricks and the unequivocal magic of metaphor into something that allows us to see a continuity between every little piece of dirt and every human bone that is always present, that is an actual astounding and overlooked truth, but is too frequently obscured by the illusion that we consent to as the collective understanding of reality? The words below were written during a period of what the psychiatric establishment considered intense mania... decide for yourself.

The trick is to be fluid like a river -- break down and return again in new form with the same elements - renewed from defeat. The trick is to remember that we grow into new shapes as we mature – like plants going to seed - shooting up and branching out -- drying up and exploding, regrowing thicker and more used to it as the years go by --sprouting wings and letting loose and never ever the same and never ever satisfied to stay put. You and me we always end up back at the same places again, and here we all are in this city of eight million faces continually dissolving and reforming itself -- breaking down and building back up like taproots and topsoil but it's all just us and like I said: it's about learning the lessons as they unfold like crumbling treasure maps or waves that knock us over -- carrying pockets of seed and scribbled words, head and mouth full of ideas and connections -- becoming the living breathing bridge between universes, conduit for the life force to flow all over us, every last one.

As we scale from macro to micro and back again we touch a form of consciousness for which there is little role in our society. "Because our maps of reality are determined by our present circumstances, we tend to lose awareness of the larger patterns of time and space. Only by gaining access to the Transcendent Other can those patterns of time and space and our role in them be glimpsed. Shamanism strives for a higher point of view, which is achieved through a feat of linguistic prowess. The shaman is one who has attained a vision of the beginnings and the endings of all things and who can communicate that vision..." (Food of the Gods, p.7)

So much of the state that gets labeled mania comes down to communication. We find messages everywhere—we are just as likely to perceive truth coming from the seedlings on our windowsills and the billboards on our streetcorners as we are from a textbook or a television. We want the world to see what we see, to know what we know, whether it is glorious or apocalyptic. Our minds are dwelling in a place where everything is speaking to us... but for our whole lives we've been told that things like this only happen in fairy tales and psych wards. In other cultures, such states are seen as necessary magic. According to Terence McKenna, the shaman journeys

"into an invisible realm in which the causality of the ordinary world is replaced with the rationale of natural magic. In this realm, language, ideas, and meaning have greater power than cause and effect. Sympathies, resonances, intentions, and personal will are linguistically magnified through poetic rhetoric. The imagination is invoked and sometimes its forms are beheld visibly. Within the magical mind-set of the shaman, the ordinary connections of the world and what we call natural laws are deemphasized or ignored... The rational, mechanistic, anti-spiritual bias of our own culture has made it impossible for us to appreciate the mind-set of the shaman. We are culturally and linguistically blind to the world of forces and interconnections clearly visible to those who have retained the Archaic[pre-industrial and preliterate] relationship to Nature. (pp. 6-8)

in this society the mystics will always live on the margins

by jacks mcnamara

a man named todd in the desert growing celery on a day with electric light
and I am a passer-through seeking some kind of truth behind the strip-mall façade of america and he is
channeling it through the minerals in his plants and we are talking under a disproportionate amount of sunlight
for november and he has known me for about 10 minutes and I can feel myself radiating some kind of energy out
through my skin and as I get totally swept away in all the plans and perceptions I am talking about he looks me
straight in the eye and says "your head is like an open funnel, isn't it, like someone just cut the top off and the
whole world pours in and you can't keep it out, can you? that must be amazing. that must be very hard. you have
a jump on the rest of us, you know? we have to work so much harder to be open and get at the wisdom of things."
a few minutes later I am talking about the icarus project and he says
"oh, you're manic-depressive, well of course, it all makes more sense now."

later we are talking about being given access to visions of the universe, access to visions of its wholeness and the
interconnected nature of love, access to a sense of time and space that allows you to discern what is and is not
important, that makes it seem silly to fear death and easy to open your arms to everything you encounter—he is
talking about getting access through years of meditation and I am talking about getting access through a few
weeks of mania—we are talking about where we are lucky and where we are not—we are talking about getting
these glimpses before you are ready to hold them in your head, when they are still so strong they can burn you,
when the frantic attempt to keep knowledge of them burning in the center of your mind sends you spinning out
into the abyss to do more work on yourself and try again...

we are talking about how this culture defines success as productivity. we are talking about how there is no
place in this society for people whose productive work cannot be measured, for people who channel spirits
and create art and roam the country spreading sparks of information and inspiration. and he says to me, so
simply: "in this society the mystics will always live on the margins." and I nod and I shake my head, thinking
how sad that is, and then my brain is flooded with a vision of driving through the desert near
Death Valley, possessed by music and the accelerating dispersal of clouds across an
iridescent sky, feeling unconnected in any way to the time and place where I was born but
completely plugged in to a time and space that has existed for millions of years, long
enough to carve the lowest valley in the western hemisphere next to 11,000 feet of
mountain and an unmeasured expanse of sky.

I wonder often who I could be if I was not born in this version of history.

I have to take medicine to fit all the realities around me in my head without exploding or disintegrating. because I cannot tune them out. I see things and they move me, hard, make me run around the globe, make me seek change, make me write furiously to have a place to put all the observations, paint furiously to have a place to put all the awe, and I don't know how anyone could do it any differently. trying to work steady jobs has always seemed like soul death to me. I can't imagine wanting to be somewhere that long. maybe I'm just young. it's not all that though. I know plenty of young folks who do just fine with a steady job and a television.

It's time to draw new lines on the map.

the map is full of boundaries. boundaries that man created. boundaries that are temporary. straight lines over curved hills. double lines between people who speak different languages. blue lines for big roads with no stop signs whose construction requires bulldozing farms and old gas stations. dashed lines for roads that pass by mountains, which are relegated to scenery now. at one point they were goddesses.

have you ever felt like a mountain was a goddess? really felt it? stood at the lip of a wide valley and looked up at the thousands of feet of rock pressing into the stars and felt deep down in your bones that this was a divine being? and have you ever had to wonder, because of a label a nasty old man in a labcoat once gave you, if you only felt this because you were exhibiting symptoms? if you would even be finding yourself in the middle of the desert at all if you didn't have some disorder that made a desperate need to leave the city walls and quit your job and take off for an unpeopled expanse of dirt seem reasonable? have you ever wondered if you would probably be in that city working behind walls if you agreed to swallow a bunch of pills? have you ever wondered why other people aren't making pilgrimages to those mountains and feeling their holiness and understanding that buying stuff has nothing to do with happiness? have you ever wondered if things would change in this big dying world if more people did that? have you ever felt a desperate, burning need to share the message, to call it out in song or write it out in words or act it out with your own naked body? have you ever wondered why this is ok for some people and pathological for others?

It is time to draw new lines on the map.

the map was made by men with measuring instruments. it was made by men with chains and money. it plots the paths people take that people before them have taken. it does not plot the paths we don't have a way to draw. it does not plot the paths that don't do well with grids. the map is all about ownership—this belongs to canada and this belongs to kansas. none of it belongs to you. the map is not about imagination. it is about defining the limits of the globe.

we need to imagine. we need to imagine a globe without limits: a planet. a planet that is part of something even larger than itself, something so big that words like stars and millenia are tiny like seeds before you can even see them, seeds underground waiting to create something enormous like a redwood out of light and air and mud and time and mystery. We are like seeds and we create words like milennia and madness that grow a world around us. We need to imagine a place for visions like that. we need to imagine an atlas where the experiences we label "psychosis" and "mania" don't get written off the map. Or quarantined to hospitals and penitentiaries.

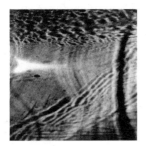 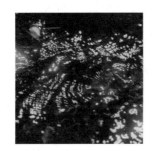 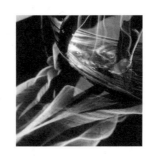 

I sit and I write all these words to you about how taking drugs isn't evil and consulting with psych doctors won't kill you. I write about learning to harness your fire. I write about consistency and follow-through and taking a sleeping pill before you get too high. And I mean it, because we live in a society that doesn't provide any guidance when we're flying or allow any crash space when we're coming back down. A society that will punish us by evicting or incarcerating us if we get too far from the one sanctioned reality: working life. A society where I honestly fear I'm likely to end up dead if I let my mind go as far into other dimensions of reality as it would like. But you know what—I miss my mania. I do. I miss feeling like my skin is so thin that the air between trees can breathe right through me and God's whispers can't help but get in my cells. I miss seeing the electricity of empty space stretch to the corners of my eyes just as clearly as the colors of music would interlace with every open road I've ever known across the dark expanse of my mind. I miss feeling millenia of human history pulse in my belly late at night. I think I really did touch on a set of truths that could help me live with a wide and peaceful mind if I could keep them with me, could help me live with a vision as limitless as the view I saw from a cliff above the sea on one of those "manic" afternoons—the ocean was silver and endless and far enough away that it became clear its waves were only skin on the surface of a body somehow at peace in endless motion, a body that opened to the horizon like truth and was no more separate from the sky than it was from me... but I had to walk back down the hill that day and drive into the city for work and eventually the moments when I seemed inseparable from the magic of the world I inhabited slipped out of my grasp and left a residue of ink on the pages of my journal and a series of questions burned into my blood.

Alternate Dimensions or Psychotic Delusions?
another dialogue from the members of The Icarus Project Website

manic depression and spirituality   By: emiko

so does anybody who's gone psychotic feel that they've touched on other dimensions? seen energies? or come closer to the divine?

i'm not so religious, but I believe everyone has an ideology through which they construct and interact with their worlds, and spirituality bleeds into this. so regardless of whether or not we're spiritual, how does having gone psychotic mesh into our worldview? it seems many feel that we're just broken, that something is simply and clearly wrong with us, and that any psychotic experience is merely an aberration. perhaps i'm naive, but I believe reality is a "collective hunch," though necessary for functioning in the world we've created. there is much more, in my opinion, than this reality. it could all be in our heads, but the unconscious is full of otherworldly phenomena. I would somehow like to deal with what happened to me (my manic episodes) in a way that doesn't reduce it to brain chemistry or conventional notions of insanity. am I delusional to think this?

Yes   By: MtMan

"So does anybody who's gone psychotic feel that they've touched on other dimensions? seen energies? or come closer to the divine?"

Yes. But then the next question is "so what?"

Once you've been there - it's designed so that you are diagnosed as being crazy, so no one would believe your insights anyways. Plus you can't stay there - eventually you come crashing down. When this happens you don't even have the mental clarity or energy to write about what you learned during your enlightenment.

Mania is enlightenment. But there is a cruel joke whereby you've been given the gift of mania for a few days, yet afterwards it's still a big "so what?" because no one will believe your insights anyways. If they find out you're on medication then you will really be ignored.

communicating with the spirits   By: eduardo

I separate the specific 'insights' that may come to me in an extended state of mania from the physical feeling of reaching another realm, and that's how I avoid the 'so what.' A physical feeling of being on the edge of known human existence in relation to birth, death, the planets, whatever, is not a 'so what'---it's a pretty cherishable thing. Explanations I may race to, in a conspiracy-theory-style moment, of details and events I may notice as if they form a logic, a sentence with a conclusion, as it were, are something else. Those pretty much have to be pricked with a pin, and yes, they don't always translate into interesting literature or artwork or what have you....never mind into a cosmological explanation. They might yield points of entry for actual investigations of existing intellectual or spiritual systems, even if through an initial misunderstanding....in any case, while it may be true that a delusional structure we invest belief in while manic mostly turns out to be useless, a feeling of the bareness or spareness of existence is, I think, not something at which to turn up one's nose. However, you can get there via other means than a BP or other psychotic episode---anemia or blood loss can do it, or even just a day going well beyond all possible expectation....Extreme physical exertion can do it, as well. I mean here to stress this experience as physical feeling that incorporates where the head goes. The heightened physical sense of being very alive is probably as close as (I think) we get to the divine, regardless of what the myths are that we receive during that state or in a more ordinary state of reception.

Consciousness Embedded in the Chemistry   By: Ng

I think that all thoughts are made up of brain chemistry and electricity. But that doesn't take away any of the magic, miracle, and beauty. Somehow, consciousness is embedded in all of that. I am a materialist in that I do think there is "stuff" outside of my body that I am perceiving (I don't just 'imagine' this keyboard and all of you). But still, in a sense I create the world, or at least an interpretation of it, based upon the input of my senses and the complex relationships I assign to different pieces of that input. My spirituality comes to a large degree from the faith that other people and animals also have consciousness. This adds a real spin to the created world in my head, because it means that my vision of the world isn't just an arbitrary construction--I'm actually communicating with other people... In communion with other spirits.

Doorways   By: icarus

Hey there-- So I'm mostly responding to Emiko's question if other people feel like they've touched other dimensions, seen energies, or become closer to the divine when manic.

Yes. I think so. And while I think that my unique chemistry might have helped me to get to those doorways sooner than I might have without it, I don't write off those experiences as simply chemical and therefore meaningless, therefore somehow unreal.

When I became manic last fall I was intensely interested in spiritual readings and Buddhism in particular. I'd begun sitting zazen and going to dharma talks and reading all kinds of books and having all kinds of realizations that accelerated the more manic I became. I developed an ability to read a book like Be Here Now or Crooked Cucumber—which I actually find a bit slow and spacey now—and have every detail connect with everything I'd ever experienced in a way that was like lightning--immediate, complete, and electric. Everything I encountered was like that: I distinctly remember sitting in my garden one night at 3 in the morning cause I just couldn't sleep and talking to god and looking at the little stones I'd placed around some of my plants that had now moved due to topography and water and immediately drawing the connection that those stones are just like our plans and our intentions that we set in the cosmos and must expect will be shifted by the greater wisdom of the universe... and on and on... and I wasn't necessarily wrong. I think a lot of the conclusions I came to and places I entered were very real. I don't think they were delusions. when I go back and read in my journals the conclusions I was coming to i'm amazed at how true my words seem, but I don't understand how I got there—it was like I had instant access to a distinct awareness of the presence of the Divine in all things, and to a rarefied kind of knowledge I didn't even know existed before--and the insights were constant and rapid and all-consuming. That's where I think the chemistry comes in.

But what do I find on the other side of that experience. Is all of it gone? No. While the insights I experienced don't vibrate daily in my blood with electric certainty, the whole time nonetheless changed me radically and is still with me. And it changed my ability to make art forever. During those months my ability to paint grew about 10 years in 2 months, to the point that old friends and new friends were shocked every time they walked in my room and didn't always believe I'd made the work myself. A year later I'm making art again that seems to be picking up where I left off, that seems to have retained the rapid growth and deluge of insights... so who knows.

mania and spirit   By: alpal

to everyone, thank you again. it is extremely nice to be able to speak in this forum, and not feel manic. normally people don't find anything to discuss out of these topics in my daily life. it is refreshing to hear so much. emiko gracias for starting it out.
I often, almost daily, will have minor episodes where everything seems unreal in a sense. I find everything spiritual, and do believe in a form of spirit. akin to native american ideals of a spirit in the earth, the wind, etc. I also grew up with Quakers who believe that there is that of god in each of us. However, it is more geared toward the kind of "do unto others as others..." thought, and not based in a multi-dimensional world way.
so, I tend to gravitate toward reality. whatever the definition may be. So what?... does affect me a lot. I find like mt man that I will have epiphanies I reach where I create something I believe mind boggling and then retract from that to find only a little inspiration. So, I tend to stay brown and safe because flights to the sun hurt too much for me.

If you could write the language that we use to discuss 'mental illness' what words would you use?

"…can't think of any specifics-it's more the way a lot of us (humans) use the language, how literally we take it, that bothers me. Like many other things, "manic depression" is just a symbol, a container, a way of organizing life so we can communicate. My uncle compared "labels" to a map - gives us a place to start, but we can go wherever we choose. It's so simple and confusing at once. Sometimes it feels like both I and the other people in my life see me as having this THING, Bipolar Disorder; it feels disconnected, not right… Structures are good as long as we realize the purpose of structure is to support freedom, not to box ourselves in. Words are tools, and like money and material possessions, I'm noticing how much we put value on the symbols rather than what's Real…" –dianalupi

" 'illness' is language. it provides prepackaged value. to be mentally ill is obviously not something to be desired, unless, of course, you're crazy. see the circular logic? to be mentally transformed, to be in the chrysalis preparatory to paradigm change, to be post-caterpillar and pre-butterfly, to be testing your wings, to be seeking transformation, to have a fundamental nature of seeking transformation, now, that's another thing. each of these descriptions is specific, in part because it is not cliché.

i have been trained as a writer. in my writing training, the teachers guided us away from the use of descriptive clichés for un-named reasons. now i think i know why. the figure of speech which once was transformative and empowering ('what is in a name? a rose, by any other name, would smell as sweet,') has become rigid with overuse, and when its stiff form is pressed against a living situation, it does violence to what is alive in the situation, alive, soft, breathing, vulnerable, new. i call this 'cookie cutter violence' but i damn well hope that, even if some people find this term useful, others will discover an alternate way of framing this depersonalizing in language!" –anon

---

These are some of the words they give us.

The definitions given below are excerpted from *Diagnostic and Statistical Manual of Mental Disorders*, Fourth Edition, 1994 (American Psychiatric Association, 1400 K Street NW, Suite 1101, Washington, DC 20005-2403 USA).

Bipolar I Disorder--Diagnostic Features (DSM-IV, p. 350)
The essential feature of Bipolar I Disorder is a clinical course that is characterized by the occurrence of one or more Manic Episodes or Mixed Episodes. Often individuals have also had one or more Major Depressive Episodes.

Bipolar II Disorder—Diagnostic Features (DSM-IV, p. 359)
The essential feature of Bipolar II Disorder is a clinical course that is characterized by the occurrence of one or more Major Depressive Episodes accompanied by at least one Hypomanic Episode. Hypomanic Episodes should not be confused with the several days of euthymia that may follow remission of a Major Depressive Episode.

"Am I the only one out there who thinks it's really creepy that folks who use mental health resources in the United States often refer to themselves as 'consumers?' Do other people know what I'm talking about here? I come across this all the time in the literature and in conversations with social workers and mental health advocates. You want some 'new language' for that one: yeeeech!
I don't like the 'consumer' label at all. From my vantage point it's about as disempowering as you can get. When I think consumer I see some drooling person sitting in front of their TV set with a coca-cola in one hand and a chicken mcnugget in the other, ashtray full of Marlboro butts and medicine bottles full of colorful pills. I'm assuming that the origins of the term can be traced to some reformist organizing campaign trying to gain more services for people with mental illnesses: like 'See, we buy things too! You better treat us with respect! Buying power is voting power!' Well that's just great, but I myself don't ever want to be referred to as a fucking 'consumer' like it's some empowering statement about my place in society. I'll take 'crazy' or 'maniac' any day over that one. Next?" –scatter

"For me it is an alchemical use of language that most pertains--that's my most positive experience of my own linguistic mental illness, involvement with that process of content transformation not only of substance but of MEANING. That's a bit different from the scientificizing, mathematizing word 'bipolar,' which suggests we're always swinging between the same two things with no variety of thought or experience---or that the variety has no life value; or the word 'mania,' which describes a state but not its content. Or 'depression,' one of the most powerful, condemning words of all, which suggests that when we see things bleakly the content of our perceptions is uniformly or exclusively irrational, or at any rate to be discounted. There's no question, for example, that relentlessly, obsessively pounding one's head into the wall (physically or figuratively) about the demise of democracy could be taken as a sign of severe depression; on the other hand, the fact that one is miserable and obsessed doesn't necessarily detract from the validity and relevance of one's observations.

Just think: when we watch a film noir from the forties, and people act all dark and obsessive and on the edge of their minds, and everyone seems kind of down, including the lighting, we're well aware that the genre was a reaction to the second world war, to the post war experience....and it's OK to drink about it, and pull guns about it, and escape into the night with Lauren Bacall about it.
Or, with Bukowski, same extended metaphor. Whereas these days, the drama is the bringing of the helpless lunatic or psycho from darkness into some divine happy light, or not being able to perform said rescue (SHINE comes to mind…)

Criteria for Major Depressive Episode DSM-IV p. 327

A. Five (or more) of the following symptoms have been present during the same 2-week period and represent a change from previous functioning; at least one of the symptoms is either (1) depressed mood or (2) loss of interest or pleasure.

1. depressed mood most of the day, nearly every day, as indicated by either subjective report (e.g., feels sad or empty) or observation made by others (e.g. appears tearful). Note: In children and adolescents, can be irritable mood.
2. markedly diminished interest or pleasure in all, or almost all, activities most of the day, nearly every day (as indicated by either subjective account or observation made by others)
3. significant weight loss when not dieting or weight gain (e.g., a change of more than 5% of body weight in a month), or decrease or increase in appetite nearly every day. Note: In children, consider failure to make expected weight gains.
4. insomnia or hypersomnia nearly every day
5. psychomotor agitation or retardation nearly every day (observable by others, not merely subjective feelings of restlessness or being slowed down)
6. fatigue or loss of energy nearly every day
7. feelings of worthlessness or excessive or inappropriate guilt (which may be delusional) nearly every day (not merely self-reproach or guilt about being sick)
8. diminished ability to think or concentrate, or indecisiveness, nearly every day (either by subjective account or as observed by others)
9. recurrent thoughts of death (not just fear of dying), recurrent suicidal ideation without a specific plan, or a suicide attempt or a specific plan for committing suicide

B. The symptoms do not meet criteria for a Mixed Episode.
C. The symptoms cause clinically significant distress or impairment in social, occupational, or other important areas of functioning.
D. The symptoms are not due to the direct physiological effects of a substance (e.g., a drug of abuse, a medication) or a general medical condition (e.g., hypothyroidism).
E. The symptoms are not better accounted for by bereavement, i.e., after the loss of a loved one, the symptoms persist for longer than 2 months or are characterized by marked functional impairment, morbid preoccupation with worthlessness, suicidal ideation, psychotic symptoms, or psychomotor retardation.

Theoretically, this is because we are a more compassionate society which cares for its people according to the latest in scientific research and terminology and in the most modern facilities with the coolest tools; but many here will agree that, put another way, we are simply all classified now for the control and comfort of someone other than ourselves, and with less regard for our individuality and expression than before. (And, lest we not forget, we are now more than ever seen as reflections of problems in the nuclear family, rather than as scarred in any way by larger social and political issues.)
So, if the language for discussing 'mental illness' is 'take your pills, get up at 7 a.m. every morning and be in bed by 10 at night, get along with your parents, don't cause trouble at work, don't take an unnatural, inordinate, presumptive interest in the way the world works or doesn't or assume you have any ability or right to influence it, watch football and ET like everyone else and be glad there's good plumbing where you live'....well, obviously, that has to be changed.....

Curiously, however, we DON'T see Hollywood making compelling, dark dramas about desperate people on the brink of disaster due to coming home with Gulf War Syndrome...that remains the purview of the military and no one else may know about it and those people aren't having those experiences. Right?
So, it is not merely a question of language, but a question of permissible referent." –eddy

77

"I don't have any alternatives to that word consumer because I fear they'd come out all ambitious-long-un-euphonious and easy to make fun of- like 'afro-american' when it was first being touted as the new 'black.' I mean I can't think of an alternative I'd want to hear in the mouths of a doctor or therapist because then, by it's very co-optedness, I wouldn't feel like it was mine but theirs. Consumer is good in a very twisted way because it lends a legitimacy and right (as in rights) in the eyes of the majority of people with their own, admittedly flawed and twisted, system of legitimacy and empowerment.

I mean hey: this is a consumer culture and in a very strange way this is the best they can do; like a child bringing you a malformed ashtray (when you don't even smoke) or a macaroni necklace: well intended, but secretly you're like -- okay, am I really gonna wear this??

(Yes I know most of US would- and we'd fuckin' rock that macramé thong we knit in art therapy, but we're dealing with the nature of language and the primacy of convenience in analogies and labels.) In other words it's the best they can do and any reform movement of labeling will, by its very nature, be unsatisfactory to most or all of us, because the descriptions we exchange as the private currency (like how I slipped in a subliminal advert [doh i did it again- my head hurts] for capitalism?) of membership would sound ridiculous coming from 'The Man.' Like white people saying word up G (and yes i am happily aware of the irony of a half-honky mc saying this)- but yo, my canine friend: they ain't us so they shouldn't talk like us.

Poetry in my mouth is pornography in theirs and all of a sudden I'm ashamed I ever used private beautiful idiosyncratic language to describe myself because it comes out with heavy clumsy wood-shop quotes, ones I can almost see and feel. I mean, I've read my 'private' records from hospitalizations - seeing myself quoted - well it's like hearing your slang in a police report.

In a way I feel bogus posting then because I can't or don't want to give you any alternative word or phrase because it would be a one-time butterfly word to describe ME and taken out of context I'd feel funny. I know I'm not fond of 'consumer' but, one, I have an almost instinctive osmotic affinity for jargon, and B (that never gets old does it) I know it's a more powerful alternative in their minds so I use it with 'them' and wince at it when I talk to Sascha or anyone else in this small but mighty tribe of reform 'mental activists' (how's that one? only problem and it's big- it presupposes a radical reform mentality and not all us 'consumers' share a burning desire for reform.) I know I do, but I'm surrounded by many people seemingly very happy with their meds and their place in the system and I don't want to disservice them by setting up some kind of bogus Black Panther and Uncle Tom dichotomy either and we all know how ridicule-ready many new-school pc terms can be, (anyone remember 'mentally challenged'- my dad used to like to say vertically challenged could be the new lazy).

But hey, just for the fuck of it we could always try- let it not be said I wasn't willing to engage in the dialogue with an indigestible chunk of monologue: iilnation, mood-confused republic, disproportionately-overmedicated, the shuffle-gaited sherpas (that one goes out to all my schizophrenic homies), manic-D (one I've actually used for quite a while, much like when upon entering a locked ward you'd find me thumping my chest with a fist and saying 'my people.'

Criteria for Manic Episode (DSM-IV, p. 332)

A. A distinct period of abnormally and persistently elevated, expansive, or irritable mood, lasting at least 1 week (or any duration if hospitalization is necessary).

B. During the period of mood disturbance, three (or more) of the following symptoms have persisted (four if the mood is only irritable) and have been present to a significant degree:

1. inflated self-esteem or grandiosity
2. decreased need for sleep (e.g., feels rested after only 3 hours of sleep)
3. more talkative than usual or pressure to keep talking
4. flight of ideas or subjective experience that thoughts are racing
5. distractibility (i.e., attention too easily drawn to unimportant or irrelevant external stimuli)
6. increase in goal-directed activity (either socially, at work or school, or sexually) or psychomotor agitation
7. excessive involvement in pleasurable activities that have a high potential for painful consequences (e.g., engaging in unrestrained buying sprees, sexual indiscretions, or foolish business investments)

C. The symptoms do not meet criteria for a Mixed Episode.

D. The mood disturbance is sufficiently severe to cause marked impairment in occupational functioning or in usual social activities or relationships with others, or to necessitate hospitalization to prevent harm to self or others, or there are psychotic features.

E. The symptoms are not due to the direct physiological effects of a substance (e.g., a drug of abuse, a medication, or other treatments) or a general medical condition (e.g., hyperthyroidism).

Hypomanic Episodes
must meet the above criteria except minimum duration is 4 days, and the mood disturbance is not severe enough to cause marked impairment in social or occupational functioning, or to necessitate hospitalization, and there are no psychotic features.
(DSM-IV, p. 338)

or 'yes-ssir my peeps.' But again I feel close to both the gadflies and agitators and the happily chemically-manipulated brethren and all the admixtures in-between who have radically different flavors of crazy than me and never, ever, want to revisit those states again. It works for them to see it as the doctors do- a dangerous thing to be eradicated. I mean, I can grasp these two things at once: loving yourself and the way you are and not liking seeing what you consider your very self-hood pathologized, but then knowing you might not survive another mixed state or morbid melancholic endless depression. Hell, it's my hardwired multi-tasking nature to easily grasp paradox, it's what makes a lot of us special- that and many other characteristics that can be, at different times, and with varying intensities, either an amazing capability or a crippling handicap (hypersensitivity anyone? that one for me is the perfect example of the double-edged 'symptom.')

Ahh logorrhea and hypergraphia my old friends-symptoms schmymptoms, get this, my favorite example of jargon in action, here's one of the side-effects of dexedrine: 'false sense of well being.' Hhhmmm, and with SSRI's that's its therapeutic effect! ya . gotta love em. I'm gone like voltron, sub-wendy lemmonfrost."

meds, from those who refused and preferred such terms as 'ex-patients,' or 'survivors.' I began using it after several conversations I had with a guy who runs an organization called 'OCTA.' That's Office of Consumer Technical Assistance. Very interesting person, who at one point had lived in one of R.D Laing's communities in the U.K.

Now, when you say the word consumption, the first image that pops into my head is a clear-cut. It's a disgusting word, and 'consumer' has the same connotation. Our humanity is reduced to our absorption of resources thereby 'feeding' the economy.

I guess what keeps it in my usage is that I don't believe in 'consuming' psych drugs, and 'feeding' the industry that has committed such a Holocaust against the Mad, anymore than I 'believe' in using toilet paper. Still I do both, and therefore I am a 'consumer' to the extent that I financially contribute to normalizing, brain damaging 'psychiatry,' and clearcutting chemical spraying 'logging.'
If I had the courage of my verbiage I'd be living in the woods, my psychosis would serve to interpret the infinitudes of the creatures, the stars, and I'd wipe my ass with dead leaves, and rinse in the river..." -Madliberator

---

Criteria for Mixed Episode (DSM-IV, p. 335)
A. The criteria are met both for a Manic Episode and for a Major Depressive Episode (except for duration) nearly every day during at least a 1-week period.
B. The mood disturbance is sufficiently severe to cause marked impairment in occupational functioning or in usual social activities or relationships with others, or to necessitate hospitalization to prevent harm to self or others, or there are psychotic features.
C. The symptoms are not due to the direct physiological effects of a substance (e.g., a drug of abuse, a medication, or other treatment) or a general medical condition (e.g., hyperthyroidism).

Cyclothymic Disorder (DSM-IV, p. 400)
A) For at least 2 years, the presence of numerous periods with hypomanic symptoms and numerous periods with depressive symptoms that do not meet criteria for a Major Depressive Episode. Note: In children and adolescents, the duration must be at least 1 year.
B) During the above 2-year period (1 year in children and adolescents), the person has not been without the symptoms in Criterion A for more than 2 months at a time.
C) No Major Depressive Episode, Manic Episode, or Mixed Episode has been present during the first 2 years of the disturbance…

"I find it so hard.....the way I police myself, my thoughts...the law book is the DSM...my own fear acts as the cops, armed by medicine. and in a way, yes, I guess I do need to be controlled. but god, what an awful thing to say. 'I need to be controlled'...it's such a hard awakening to see that your own unbridled freedom bites the head of your personal power." -Lizzening

"This forum, this project, the creation of a new language with which we can speak and think about madness, is so important. The post above about the word 'consumer' struck me because I have found myself using it over the last year or so, as an attempt at 'political correctness' at work (I'm a social worker) while my own preferred term in my personal life is Madness, (I'm Mad) not to be confused with sickness.
I think the term 'consumer' began to be applied to people who 'consumed' mental health services, to distinguish those in the anti-psychiatry movement who nevertheless continued to take

"i don't know. i think the world is trembling and reacting to something very large and very wrong. i think some people are calling this bipolar. i think this country is bipolar. look at the history of the 20th century. we actually define decades as 'The Roaring Twenties' and 'The Great Depression.' we've just been through another one of these 'hypomanic' episodes with the tech boom of the nineties. and how does our country react when the bubble bursts? go to war. put on more lipstick. try to feel powerful.

i think if we were all outside planting things instead of spending our lives in cars and arguing with our cell phone providers, we might just be called 'deep' instead of 'depressed' or 'bipolar.' " -Daedalus

MY THOUGHTS & FEELINGS ARE NOT DISEASES

by Madliberator (Tim)

If I had a dime for every time they said, its just like diabetes...

I grew up with a very, very, manic mother. So disturbed that she finally was locked up in the state institution and I was whisked off into foster care...but that's another story. I can remember her giving me the NAMI line, seems around the time "bipolar" became the fashionable terminology: "Mental illnesses are brain disorders." I swallowed it whole, and by the time I was 15 was chasing it down with fistful of Depakote and Prozac, hold the Haldol if you please. It seems dreadfully easy to assume that because my mother and I experience very similar thoughts and feelings, that they must be a genetic disorder. But, hold the phone, I grew up away from my father, yet we read the same books, have the same anarchist tendencies, and look alike. Why is that not considered a disease? Because the things I share with my mother are socially undesirable. So why is it that when we feel sad, or ecstatic to the point of hallucinations, we go to a doctor?

Medical authority is likely the least questioned authority there is. We are distressed and want it to stop. We are told that pills are the answer. I'll be the first to admit that they "work." I took Lithium and Wellbutrin this morning, and will be taking Lithium and Seroquel in a few hours. All that to keep me bottled up. Folks, the way I see it is, we ain't sposed to be livin' this way. Industrial society is too much. Especially the modern American version. I mean, it's weird right? When you find yourself at three am wandering the endless halls of WAL-MART to the sound of billy ray cyrus recycled through kenny g and remixed by jazzy-jeff, fluorescent lights burning your eyes and buzzing, and you notice that all the food is in boxes, neatly measured, and everything is disposable—remember, we are not supposed to be living this way. And it can't last long.

Maybe we're just extra sensitive; our madness gives us some special insight into the world. I mean think about it, most everything these days is an ultra complicated mental construct. In our delusional states Sascha, and I'm sure most of us, experience the feeling like everything has some hidden meaning. It's not that we're wrong, it's just that others don't share that interpretation. Seriously. Somewhere Sascha was talking about thinking there was some hidden language under the every day language, and there is!! A multitude of languages. Course, if you're trying to hold down a steady job, pay bills, etc, you'd better stick with everyday language, cause when you start looking at the others...well y'all know...its playing with fire. But it truly is brilliance folks!!! That billboard is related to what your friend said that night, they are trying to manipulate you with the radio, you do have special powers, and of course, the government is out to get all of us.

Usually these things are really exaggerated, but it's still there. I'm a social worker, and here in Oregon the state is broke, so they have been cutting all kinds of stuff. Many of my clients are Mad, and even if diagnosed with schizophrenia have a tough time getting in to see a doctor or let alone actually getting a prescription filled. The drug companies dole out samples to the clinics, y'all know how it works, when they run out... Bedlam. I think it's our responsibility to do more than just dope ourselves normal. We are the harbingers of the future. Look at the world around us!! This is not how we are meant to live. My girlfriend's in Mexico right now, she tells me that when the floods come, the garbage just floats by, children playing in the water. I have word from Argentina that when NAFTA and company let those huge agribusinesses down there, the GM plants were designed so they wouldn't produce seeds, forcing folks to become dependent, but alas, its an old song, and you've heard it a thousand times. It's natural for us to be depressed in this world!!! I guess we just do what we can. I just hope you all remember, you don't have a disease. If you have to take a fistful of pills to keep yourself alive and out of trouble, then I'd be the first to get you a glass of water, and then I'd hold your hand and say, "it's not you, you're not sick, it took a few thousand years for it to get this way, you're just someone who can't help but notice, you feel it in your soul."

Sweet Potatoes and Little Ladders in the Sky: Thanks and Explanations

To get this reader done we basically shut ourselves away from the rest of the world for two months and camped out at Sascha's mom's house in the middle of the woods in the Hudson Valley of New York. (We cannot thank her enough for her home and all her support.) We worked on it every day, usually for a bunch of hours, especially in the last month. The last few weeks we didn't do anything else. Literally. But we treated ourselves right and used our grant money to pay for good food at the local co-op (even though it was 45 minutes away). We ate more sweet potatoes than you can imagine, lots of kale, kamut pancakes with maple syrup for breakfast and miso soup with tahini and sesame oil for lunch. When we weren't sitting in front of the computer we were in the kitchen cooking or giving each other back rubs and wandering outside to play in the snow and stare up at the stars in the night sky. We tried our best to keep our manic minds sleeping eight hours a night. And we took care of each other. This has been a really intense experience for both of us - we've gotten to know each other really well and we've talked so much about our childhoods, our psychoses, our big old dreams, our lost loves, and all our ghosts. We cracked each other up constantly and forevermore will be full of language and jokes that no one else will understand, in the way that happens when two people spend too much time together. All the crying we did on each other's shoulders, all the sentences we finished for each other before they had time to leave our mouths—all of that stuff is hidden inside this reader, nestled subtly between the lines even though you might not be able to see it. **This was truly a labor of love.**

We want people to learn to take care of themselves so they can be bad-ass beautiful uncompromising human beings. We want to build little ladders into the sky and shatter myths—like this one: You can't be creative on Lithium. Wrong. We created this entire reader in 2 months, worked at it feverishly and with ever expanding levels of understanding and an unbelievable current of ideas flowing—and we are both on Lithium, and a couple other drugs between us. This is the most sustainably creative we have ever been. Both of us agree wholeheartedly that this is the most amazing thing we've ever done in our lives. And it never would have happened if we didn't try so hard to be good to our bodies and souls.

Although we're ambitious, there are lots of things that are not in this reader because our superhuman powers seem to run out after midnight. We're already thinking about everything we need to get in the next version… hopefully a real book…but first we need to find time and money to print it. So e-mail us your ideas of what we should include and fix. And if you think this project is worth it, help us figure out how to get the support to make that happen. This printing is 1000 copies and we're going to photocopy the rest ourselves as we go along.

There are so many people to thank we cannot even hope to cover them all, but we'll try. First off, Anita Altman for support at every step, and Gil Kulick for being good to her and good to us. We could never have done this without the help of The Dobkin Family Foundation and FJC. The website itself would not be usable if weren't for Ryan Johnson, world's most interesting webmaster and Jacks' much loved friend (no matter how much we drive each other nuts…) Thanks for last minute psychological guidance from Nicole Breck and Elizabeth Wayne. Thanks to those who sheltered us on our weekend trips to the city: Jennifer Bleyer, Todd and Eva, Arrow and Kat and Felix, Sarah Quinter, many more to come…Thanks to Bluestockings Bookstore for a warm place to gather in the middle of Winter and Brooke Lehman for being so supportive and sexy. Thanks to Todd Chandler for computer help and a fabulous soundtrack. Jolie Holland was our unofficial theme music for the winter. Fountain House has provided enormous inspiration, as have innumerable books and websites and magazines. Thanks to all the people who have taken care of us when we're in bad places—Jacks sends a huge thank you to the homies at 2762 Folsom who cooked her food and dragged her to the shrink when things were dire, and prevented The Icarus Project from crashing before it even got off the ground. (Images: Thank you everyone, from Leonardo Davinci to The Curious George Collective, for contributing pieces of aesthetic excellence that will comfort the mentally ill and absolutely fantastic all over the world. "Crazy," on p. 15, is from Kika Kat's zine *Half-Wild*. "Mania," on p. 25, is from Dalia's zine *Open 24 Hours*—and we owe a BIG thank you to her because we used her art all over—on this page as a matter of fact. "Blue Jay Way" is from John Ellis' zine *Vacancy*. If you want contact info for these folks, let us know. Cover art is by Jacks.)

Thank You to all the amazing, inspiring, brave, hilarious, and thoroughly beautiful members of our website who make us glad to be alive and contributing our little efforts at changing the world. Keep the dialogue going!

And a special Fourth Edition thank you to: Will Hall of the Freedom Center who co-authored the new crisis and suicide pieces and is one of the most amazing modern shamans we know; Madigan who's coordinating the crazies in NYC; everyone everywhere who's helped to make our tours and speaking events incredible; Kevin Loecke and all the folks who helped pull of one hell of an artshow in December; Tom at First Impressions for being a wonderful printer on the first three editions; and The Ittleson Foundation and all our other donors for their generous support.

Postscript and Reintroduction to the 5th Printing

by Jacks McNamara, May 2006

It is Spring 2006, 2 years after Sascha and I self-published the first 1000 copies of this barely-proofread zine/book, threw them in the back of my truck, and launched into a guerrilla speaking tour of bookstores, infoshops, colleges, community centers, mental health clinics, and activist houses across the country. I have just finished re-reading the text while sitting on the same couch where we wrote it in 2 months of unbelievable immersion. I am struck by what a beginning this little volume proved to be, and by how deeply it reflects our personal passions, prejudices, privileges, and fears as individuals with a limited understanding of our own mental health and the context that shapes it. We created the first version of this book in a manic spirit of compiling all the questions we had been trying to figure out and spilling all the paradoxes and insights we had been gaining along the way. After reading through these pages I am left with images of inspiration and isolation; the bipolar person as a brilliant, alienated character struggling against society and his/her own potentially inevitable, biological madness.

I am amazed by the lack of attention we paid to the formative influences of childhood, family, environment, trauma, spiritual crisis, addiction, race, class, and privilege. I am struck by our adamant independence, our deep mistrust of authority, and our fear of our own insanity. Our framework for representing our emotional extremes reflects who we were at the time we wrote this: two privileged, creative, educated white kids who had access to the western medical system at a young age, lived through wild adventures and terrible mental breakdowns, got diagnosed with a major mental illness, took medication, and were terrified of enduring such suffering again. We did not know anyone who had successfully managed a similar craziness in the long-term without the compromises of psychiatry, and we did not have a diverse community of peers who struggled with the same baffling states of consciousness. Our response to the conventional narrative of "mental illness" was shaped more by our reactions to authority than by an identification with alternative understandings shared by our peers or developed by our elders. Though we had a lot of internal resistance to the medical model that blames everything on biology and treats everything with drugs, we still feared it might end up being right, and that our madness would recur independent of the families who raised us, the lifestyle choices we made, the alternative treatments we tried, the seasons of the year, the substances we consumed, the traumas we'd endured, the relationships we developed, or much of anything else.

Since then, we have learned so much more about all the different ways people experience and treat mental crisis. We have a wide network of mad friends all over the place. We know people who've lived without meds for 28 years and we know people who swear lithium has saved their lives for the last 20. We've read books, participated in workshops, tried new spiritual practices, experimented with martial arts, written zines, taken herbs, travelled back and forth across the country, and had so many conversations. We've been given all kinds of new language, new friends, new guides, and new hope. We have suffered and been crazy as hell and broken hearts and made messes and yet we're still going and we're still best friends. Our worlds keep getting wider and wider, and The Icarus Project manages to reach further and further.

In Autumn 2005 I decided to take a break from full-time work organizing the project to attend to my own health and recovery. After a few whirlwind years of growth, insanity, and tons of Icarus activities, from organizing art shows and redesigning our website to writing grants and leading workshops, my body had reached its limit and I developed a crippling rash in reaction to lithium. In April 2005 I began working with a homeopath, a highly trained natural healer, to get off the toxic medications and start listening to my soul. My life has changed immensely. Layers upon layers of trauma, grief, tumult, and truth started to erupt from their submersion behind the filters of workaholism, psych drugs, and alcohol. The resulting chaos got me into 12-step recovery, where I have finally become willing to take an honest look at my substance abuse, my family history, my thinking patterns, and the many factors beyond biology that contribute to my craziness and disrupt my best attempts at a sane existence.

These days my life is a lot humbler and closer to the earth. I have moved into a collective farm in the country with Sascha and other friends. I work with a homeopath and a shaman as my primary health care providers. I am sober and med-free. My hours are filled with tending goats, planting seeds, teaching art, taking care of children, cooking food with my friends, going to 12-step meetings, writing and facilitating workshops with The Icarus Project, and learning to love and trust the people around me. I make a concerted effort to accept my limitations and attend to my basic needs – not because an authority told me I must, but because I am listening to my body and trusting the people who have walked this path before me. My basic needs seem to be something like: getting to bed early, eating regular nourishing meals, meditating daily, working a reasonable amount, asking for help, taking breaks, being honest, staying in touch with my healers, depending on my community, developing routine, making space for creation, accepting my mistakes, and following through on my commitments. I still struggle, I still fear, and I still resist, but something in my core feels manageable and solid in a way I have never experienced before. I have made a real commitment to waking all the way up. Each day I try to surrender a little more. The ideal of balance and wellness seems possible if I work towards it in a gradual way and call on my guides for help. I am not giving up.

Epilogue to the 10ᵗʰ Edition

So much has changed in the nine years since we originally published this book that we both wonder sometimes if our lives are a movie or a dream. The Icarus Project is no longer fueled by the obsessive energy of two people working at a frenzied pace and holding it all together with lithium and duct tape. These days the project is supported by a network of madfolks and allies all over the world. Last Fall we celebrated our tenth anniversary with art shows, performance nights, and skillshares on both coasts. Our publications have been translated into Spanish, French, German, Italian, Hebrew, and Croatian. People are using Icarus materials in college classrooms and hatching plans for Madness Studies as an academic discipline. Our posters and info sheets are handed out as materials to youth advocates and peer specialists around the country. There are local Icarus inspired groups in places as far flung as North Dakota and India.

One of the most powerful expressions of the maturing of our community is the way that so many of our Icarista comrades are becoming healers of different kinds: social workers, acupuncturists, drama therapists, body workers, herbalists... Others have emerged as leaders in activism and media. Will Hall went on to found Madness Radio, a bunch of Icaristas blog on Robert Whitaker's Mad in America website, and Ken Rosenthal created the poetic documentary Crooked Beauty about Jacks' life & art. Some core Icarus organizers have recently joined an intergenerational group of mad movement leaders brainstorming about alternative approaches to psychosis and reestablishing a network of safe houses and sanctuaries across North America. These are exciting times.

One of the many things we didn't realize when we started Icarus was that we had elders and allies. In recent years we've been learning about all the movements and treatment modalities related to radical ideas of mental health that got buried under the rise of biopsychiatry in the 1980s. Sascha's been studying things like the history of Humanistic and Transpersonal Psychology, Gestalt Therapy, and Psychodrama, and envisioning a larger social justice movement that captures the feeling of spirit and collectivity that he's found in some Yoga communities. Jacks has been reading about decolonization as a paradigm for uprooting oppression and restoring balance to the earth and its peoples. Jacks' current organizing is greatly shaped by learning from and collaborating with movements like disability justice that are grounded in the leadership of people of color, queers, and folks of differing ability. We've both been training as healers in modalities like generative somatics and process work, and we've both, in our own ways, been exploring how individual and collective trauma shapes experiences of emotional distress.

One of the lingering questions we're always left with is how to understand if the term bipolar is even still useful, given all these new viewpoints on the causes and construction of "mental illness." Our political critique of the biopsychiatric model has left us questioning the whole nature of the term. One of the original goals of Icarus was to create new language for our experiences. When we started this journey together we used the language of "manic depression" and "bipolar disorder" as a shorthand that made some sense and was easily recognized in our culture. The birth of our community in 2002 corresponded with an explosion in the rise of "bipolar" diagnosis—in many children as well as adults—fueled by the marketing of a new class of profitable anti-psychotic drugs as "mood stabilizers." The diagnostic criteria kept getting widened and widened to the point of absurdity, and bipolar seems to be the trendy diagnosis of the day, often replacing older diagnoses like schizophrenia and ADHD. Since the early days of Icarus we've met so many people for whom "bipolar" was an oppressive and incorrect label; often these folks seemed to be dealing with the effects of long trauma histories or eccentric personalities, and conventional treatments for bipolar just made everything worse. Shortly after the first edition of *Navigating the Space* was published, we widened the scope of our community, from "by and for people with bipolar disorder" to "by and for people with bipolar disorder *and related madness*" and eventually "by and for people living with and/or affected by experiences that are often diagnosed and labeled as psychiatric conditions." We've continually tried to open space for as many people as possible to find a home or at least a resonant analysis in Icarus. From the beginning we've been interested in developing adequately complex frameworks for liberation and self-determination, encouraging people to discard what doesn't work for them and define themselves.

And yet the two of us have personally had really complicated evolving relationships with this idea of "bipolar disorder." At times we've tried to reject it completely, but ten years after starting the Icarus Project, it's seeming useful and specific. Both of us are back on mood stabilizing meds after a lot of attempts to reduce or go off them, and we're doing really well: grounded and present, engaged in the world, passionate about our writing, art, and creative organizing work. After all the recurring crises and miraculous moments, we keep finding that some of our experiences just don't make sense through another lens. We seem to be in this group of "core responders" – folks with the classic symptoms of Bipolar I – who seem to do the best in the long term on standard drugs like lithium. This group is only about 20% of those diagnosed on the bipolar spectrum. This is a really unpopular viewpoint in the radical mental health movements we're part of. In recent years groundbreaking and hopeful research has been coming out by folks like Robert Whittaker and Paris Williams that provides convincing evidence that many people recover completely from psychosis and other psychological crises without medications, and often do better in the long term if they never take them at all. We want this to be true for everyone. But most of this research focuses specifically on anti-psychotic drugs and anti-depressants, on first-break psychosis and depression, and almost never mentions folks with chronic recurrence, and/or folks who respond really well to the classic mood stabilizers. Our friends in the movement – psychiatrists who specialize in getting folks off meds, social workers who've spent years running non-coercive safe houses - admit to us in whispered voices that they've rarely seen people who fit the core diagnosis of Bipolar I come down off serious mania or stay well over the long term without the drugs. It's hard to know what to think – when do you accept something as part of you, or when do you fight again and again to overcome it? What exactly does recovery mean for us, and does recovery go far enough, or is our goal personal and collective transformation? We hope you'll be part of the conversation.

mad love

Jacks and Sascha, February 2013

Other Icarus Project Publications

Since the publication of *Navigating the Space Between Brilliance and Madness* in 2004, members of The Icarus Project have collaborated on numerous zines and books, including the 3 highlighted in the next two pages. All are available for free download on our website, or can be ordered in print from AK Press. Please get the word out by buying your own copies, giving them to your friends, donating copies to your library, asking your local independent bookstores to carry them, blogging about them, writing reviews, organizing reading groups, sharing them with your healthcare practitioners, and suggesting them to your professors. We are always open to feedback and suggestions - email us at info@theicarusproject.net.

Harm Reduction Guide to Coming Off Psychiatric Drugs

This guide brings together the best information we've discovered and lessons we've learned at The Icarus Project and the Freedom Center. It is not intended to persuade anyone to stop taking psychiatric medications, but instead aims to educate people about

their options if they decide to explore going off.

In a culture polarized between the pro-medication propaganda of pharmaceutical companies on the one hand, and the anti-medication agenda of some activists on the other, we offer a harm-reduction approach to help people make their own decisions. We also present ideas and information for people who decide to stay on or reduce their medications.

Many people do find psychiatric drugs helpful and choose to continue taking them: even with the risks, this may be a better option given someone's situation and circumstances. At the same time, psychiatric drugs carry great dangers and can sometimes do terrible harm, even becoming bigger problems than the conditions they were prescribed to treat. Too often, people who need help getting off psychiatric drugs are left without guidance, and medication decisions can feel like finding your way through a labyrinth. We need honest information that widens the discussion, and we hope this guide helps people trust themselves more and take better care of one another.

Research guidance was provided by a 14-member health professional Advisory Board comprised of medical doctors, nurses, psychologists and acupuncturists. More than 20 other collaborators with direct experience with medications were involved in developing and editing.

Mindful Occupation: Rising Up Without Burning Out

Last year, a group of us who have years of experience practicing peer-based community mental health support got together to compile a manual for organizers and participants in the #occupy movement. This is what came out of our work.

We believe that there is an urgent need to talk publicly about the relationship between social injustice and our mental health. We believe that we need to start redefining what it actually means to be mentally healthy, not just on an individual level, but on collective, communal, and global levels.

We know that many people at Occupy sites around the country are struggling to figure out how to build spaces of support and healing. We also know that police violence and the stresses of street protest can have very real mental, emotional, and energetic effects that are all too often not taken seriously.

Our aim with this booklet is to stimulate discussion, raise awareness, provide support, contribute to maintaining a more sustainable movement, and lay the foundation for the next stage of the movement. We want it to be a living document: open to revisions and remakes. We also hope this helps start conversations. Many people are doing amazing healing work within and around the Occupy movement – street medics, health professionals, bodyworkers, herbalists, energetic medicine practitioners, radical therapists and social workers, and others. We want to facilitate more discussions and get the word out about more good practices and techniques.

Image Credits: Sarah Quinter, inside front cover. Dr. Seuss dictionary, pages 2, 33, 34, 19, 45, 51, 57, 60. Dalia Shevin p. 7, 81. Becky Cloonan, p. 38. Sophie Crumb, p. 50. Trish Tripp, small door p. 53, Geena, the dream person, p. 53. Bec Young p. 74. Jacks McNamara p.3, 4, 71, 72, 73, 80, and many more odds and ends. **Big 10th edition thanks** to: Traci Picard, our generous proofreader. Anita and Gil for once again allowing us to use their house in the woods to finish this book. All the artists that have contributed new art to this edition, and made art for Icarus over the years. Everyone who's used this guide in their reading groups and given us feedback to make it better. To all the members of The Icarus Project, especially those of who have stepped up to help by moderating forums, facilitating groups, organizing events, distro-ing publications, becoming friends, keeping each other alive.